The Process of Child Therapy

Formulated by the
Committee on Child Psychiatry

Group for the Advancement of Psychiatry

BRUNNER/MAZEL *Publishers* • New York

This is #111, the fifth in the Volume XI series of publications by the Group for the Advancement of Psychiatry.

Library of Congress Cataloging in Publication Data

Main entry under title:

The Process of child therapy.

   Includes bibliographical references and
index.
   1. Child psychotherapy. I. Group for the
Advancement of Psychiatry. Committee on Child
Psychiatry. [DNLM: 1. Psychotherapy—In
infancy and childhood. WS 350.2 P963]
RJ504.P74   1982   618.92'8914   82-45469
ISBN 0-87630-310-6
ISBN 0-87630-311-4 (pbk.)

Published by
BRUNNER/MAZEL, INC.
19 Union Square West
New York, New York 10003

MANUFACTURED IN THE UNITED STATES OF AMERICA

For all those, of whatever discipline, who are learning
and developing their therapeutic skills with children

PREFACE

In this report, we have tried to do something that has not been done before but which very much needed to be done. We have looked at the process of treatment both in theory and in practice, microscopically and macroscopically, historically and currently. We have tried to look at the "meaning" of what happens during the therapeutic encounter and the way phenomena are shaped by the milieu, the participants, the language used, and that numinous quality, "the healing power," that brings about change for the better. Finally, in order to bring the examination down to earth, we have scrutinized the process in dyadic, group, family, and community therapy, in behavior, drug, peer, and collaborative therapy, attempting to assess the influence of numbers, attitudes, and medication. From the developmental point of view, which is what child psychiatry is about, the report attempts to follow the changes in the therapeutic process during different phases of therapy, and considers, as well, the changes brought about by those who supervise that process.

STATEMENT OF PURPOSE

THE GROUP FOR THE ADVANCEMENT OF PSYCHIATRY has a membership of approximately 300 psychiatrists, most of whom are organized in the form of a number of working committees. These committees direct their efforts toward the study of various aspects of psychiatry and the application of this knowledge to the fields of mental health and human relations.

Collaboration with specialists in other disciplines has been and is one of GAP's working principles. Since the formation of GAP in 1946 its members have worked closely with such other specialists as anthropologists, biologists, economists, statisticians, educators, lawyers, nurses, psychologists, sociologists, social workers, and experts in mass communication, philosophy, and semantics. GAP envisages a continuing program of work according to the following aims:

1. To collect and appraise significant data in the fields of psychiatry, mental health, and human relations
2. To reevaluate old concepts and to develop and test new ones
3. To apply the knowledge thus obtained for the promotion of mental health and good human relations

GAP is an independent group, and its reports represent the composite findings and opinions of its members only, guided by its many consultants.

THE PROCESS OF CHILD PSYCHIATRY was formulated by the Committee on Child Psychiatry which acknowledges on page xv the participation of others in the preparation of this report. The members of this committee are listed below. The following pages list the members of the other GAP committees as well as additional membership categories and current and past officers of GAP.

Othilda M. Krug, Cincinnati, Ohio

Robert L. Leopold, Philadelphia, Pa.
Alan I. Levenson, Tucson, Ariz.
Ruth W. Lidz, Woodbridge, Conn.
Maurice E. Linden, Philadelphia, Pa.
Earl A. Loomis, Jr., Greenport, N.Y.
Reginald S. Lourie, Chevy Chase, Md.

Jeptha R. MacFarlane, Garden City, N.Y.
John A. MacLeod, Cincinnati, Ohio
Leo Madow, Philadelphia, Pa.
Sidney G. Margolin, Denver, Colo.
Peter A. Martin, Southfield, Mich.
Ake Mattsson, New York, N.Y.
David Mendell, Houston, Tex.
Mary E. Mercer, Nyack, N.Y.
James G. Miller, Louisville, Ky.

John E Nardini, Washington, D.C.
Joseph D. Noshpitz, Washington, D.C.

Lucy D. Ozarin, Bethesda, Md.

Bernard L. Pacella, New York, N.Y.
Norman L. Paul, Boston, Mass.
Marvin E. Perkins, Roanoke, Va.
Charles A. Pinderhughes, Bedford, Mass.
Seymour Pollack, Los Angeles, Calif.

David N. Ratnavale, Chevy Chas, Md.
Walter Reich, Rockville, Md.
Harvey L. P. Resnik, College Park, Md.
W. Donald Ross, Cincinnati, Ohio
Lester H. Rudy, Chicago, Ill.
George E. Ruff, Philadelphia, Pa.
A. John Rush, Dallas, Tex.

David S. Sanders, Los Angeles, Calif.
Donald Scherl, Brooklyn, N.Y.
Kurt O. Schlesinger, San Francisco, Calif.
Calvin F. Settlage, Sausalito, Calif.
Charles Shagass, Philadelphia, Pa.
Albert J. Silverman, Ann Arbor, Mich.
Justin Simon, Berkeley, Calif.
Kendon W. Smith, Valhalla, N.Y.
Benson R. Snyder, Cambridge, Mass.
David A. Soskis, Bala Cynwyd, Pa.
Jeanne Spurlock, Washington, D.C.
Tom G. Stauffer, White Plains, N.Y.

Brandt F. Steele, Denver, Colo.
Eleanor A. Steele, Denver, Colo.
Rutherford B. Stevens, New York, N.Y.
Alan A. Stone, Cambridge, Mass.
Robert E. Switzer, Trevose, Pa.

Perry C. Talkington, Dallas, Tex.
Graham C. Taylor, Montreal, Canada
Prescott W. Thompson, Beaverton, Oreg.
Harvey J. Tompkins, New York, N.Y.
Lucia E. Tower, Chicago, Ill.
Joseph P. Tupin, Sacramento, Calif.
John A. Turner, San Francisco, Calif.

Montague Ullman, Ardsley, N.Y.
Gene L. Usdin, New Orleans, La.

Warren T. Vaughan, Jr., Portola Valley,
Calif.

Robert S. Wallerstein, San Francisco, Calif.
Andrew S. Watson, Ann Arbor, Mich.
Bryant M. Wedge, Washington, D.C.
Joseph B. Wheelwright, Kentfield, Calif.
Robert L. Williams, Houston, Tex.
Paul Tyler Wilson, Bethesda, Md.
Sherwyn M. Woods, Los Angeles, Calif.

Stanley F. Yolles, Stony Brook, N.Y.

Israel Zwerling, Philadelphia, Pa.

LIFE MEMBERS
C. Knight Aldrich, Charlottesville, Va.
Bernard Bandler, Cambridge, Mass.
Leo H. Bartemeier, Baltimore, Md.
Walter E. Barton, Hartland, Vt.
Ivan C. Berlien, Coral Gables, Fla.
Murray Bowen, Chevy Chase, Md.
O. Spurgeon English, Narberth, Pa.
Dana L. Farnsworth, Belmont, Mass.
Stephen Fleck, New Haven, Conn.
Jerome Frank, Baltimore, Md.
Edward O. Harper, Cleveland, Ohio
Margaret M. Lawrence, Pomona, N.Y.
Harold I. Lief, Philadelphia, Pa.
Judd Marmor, Los Angeles, Calif.
Karl A. Menninger, Topeka, Kans.
Lewis L. Robbins, Glen Oaks, N.Y.
Mabel Ross, Sun City, Ariz.

COMMITTEE ACKNOWLEDGMENTS

The Committee on Child Psychiatry of the Group for the Advancement of Psychiatry formulated a major portion of *The Process of Child Therapy* under the chairmanship of Joseph Fischhoff.

E. James Anthony, Ake Mattsson, and Virginia Wilking, though not members of the Committee now, were members during the writing of *Process* and made important contributions. The Committee lost a wise and warm member when Exie Welsch died. She will be missed by all who were fortunate enough to have known her.

Howard Hunt was the consultant on behavior therapy. Four GAP Ginsberg Fellows—Nina Kessler, David Oldham, Betty Pfefferbaum, and Norberto Rodriquez—contributed significantly to the report. Grateful acknowledgement is also made to the many GAP members who contributed comments and suggestions that have been incorporated into this report.

TABLE OF CONTENTS

Preface vii
Statement of Purpose ix
Committee Acknowledgments xv
Introduction xix

1 The Meaning of Process 3

2 The History of Child Treatment in Western
   Culture 9

3 Basic Ingredients of the Therapeutic Situation 47

4 Who Heals Disturbed Children? 61

5 Dimensions of the Therapeutic Situation 81

6 Phenomenology, Transaction, and Process 89

7 The Developmental Stages 121

8 Dyadic Psychotherapies: The Therapeutic Process 149

9 The Process of Behavior Therapy 155

10 Psychopharmacology 171

11 Family Therapy 177

12 Group Therapy 187

Therapeutic Requirements of Any Milieu 193

Collaborative Therapy with Children 199

Index 213

INTRODUCTION

Process is a fundamental fact of our experience. We are in
the present; the present is always shifting; it is derived from
the past; it is shaping the future; it is passing into the future.
This is process, and in the universe, it is an inexorable
fact . . . why should there be process? Surely the satisfactory answer must embody an understanding of the interweaving of change and permanence, each required by the
other. This interweaving is a primary fact of experience.

A. N. Whitehead[1]

In this fourth monograph on the diagnosis and treatment of
psychological disorders in children, the Group for the Advancement of Psychiatry's Committee on Child Psychiatry
continues its dialogue on process which began with the publication of *The Diagnostic Process in Child Psychiatry*,[2] and continued in *Psychopathological Disorders in Childhood*,[3] and *From
Diagnosis to Treatment*.[4] The publication of those volumes led
us, inevitably, to a consideration of the *process* of child therapy. This volume is a result of that consideration.

For children and adolescents who need treatment, we have
considered the process of treatment by identification of its
roots, of the persons involved, of the stages of development
at which children and adolescents are seen in therapy, of its
phenomenology, and of its several dimensions. The continuing development of all aspects of process gives a certain
fluidity to this report: The phenomena of movement and
change are stressed.

An historical framework gives us many moments in which
we can "stop time"—look at the process of child therapy—even
though the process of change with its movement is always

apparent. We too are part of history and will be seen in the future as not too far from Comenius* but closer to Hug-Helmuth,** moving backward while the historical process moves forward.

This report will be selective. It is not a compendium and will not be all things to everyone. It is meant to consider the *who* of the process of treatment and the *what* but not the *how*.

In the course of a natural concern with developmental process, recapitulation of the species occurs. A change in persona is part of the process; development changes the process of child therapy; the process of treatment makes that development happen.

This report does not deal with the truth but with whatever things are true, whoever the healer, wherever the transaction, whatever the particular dimension of the process of therapy. The process of child therapy can be seen as developmental: There is a point at which the process begins, a point through which the process evolves, and a point toward which it proceeds. It then passes into the future of the child or adolescent being treated.

Students in the field of child therapy should gain from this report a fuller understanding of the nuances of psychological treatment, often so obscured by conflicting theory, detailed technical considerations, and sometimes impenetrable jargon. We have deliberately stayed away from structure because it brings a plethora of theory. Our belief is not only that treatment can be best taught through a consideration of process but that process, as both Heraclitus and Whitehead affirmed, crosses the span of many thousands of years. The process of therapeutic becoming, itself, contains objects, events, entities, conditions, and structures that can be or have

*John Amos Comenius (1592-1670), Bishop of the Protestant community of the Moravian Brethren.
**Hermine von Hug-Hellmuth, a lay analyst and the first woman admitted to full membership in the Vienna Psychoanalytic Society.

been abstracted from it. The key question, we believe, is whether we therapists can become completely aware of the ever-changing and flowing reality of this process, and then conceptualize from our awareness. We believe we can and this report will demonstrate how it can be done.

References

1. Whitehead, A. N. *Modes of Thought*. New York: Macmillan, 1938.
2. Group for the Advancement of Psychiatry. *The Diagnostic Process in Child Psychiatry*. New York: Group for the Advancement of Psychiatry, 1957.
3. Group for the Advancement of Psychiatry. *Psychopathological Disorders in Childhood: Theoretical Considerations and a Proposed Classification*. New York: Group for the Advancement of Psychiatry, 1966.
4. Group for the Advancement of Psychiatry. *From Diagnosis to Treatment*. New York: Group for the Advancement of Psychiatry, 1973.

THE PROCESS OF CHILD THERAPY

1

THE MEANING OF PROCESS

Process is a fundamental part of experience for adults and children. The therapeutic process therefore is a fundamental of therapy. With children, this process must be defined and described with the care and exactitude that befit a grammar of science. In this report we scrutinize and use the experience of process in child therapy.

We note philosopher Whitehead's definition of "process" is not dissimilar from the one furnished by standard dictionaries. For example, Webster's *New World Dictionary* says:

> *Process*: A continuing development over the course of time involving many changes; a particular method of doing something generally involving a number of steps or operations.

The experience of process can therefore be said to include the sense of development, of continuity, of time—past, present, and future—in short, both a sense of permanence and a sense of change. Moreover, segments of process become separate stages or operations.

Process may be viewed as the dynamic interaction of all the phenomenological aspects of the therapy, encompassing all overt as well as covert interactional expressions of feelings, thoughts, and actions occurring over time. The "interactional" dimension need not always imply the physical encounter of either the therapist or the child, as either may be "interacting" with great intensity with the other in fantasy even before the actual therapy begins. Moreover, it is one of

3

the aims of treatment that the therapeutic process continue even after the final session.

Process also refers to intrapsychic as well as transactional events. The child in therapy continues to develop and may have corrective learning experiences in the course of therapy. The internal changes which may be evidenced by nonverbal as well as verbal expressions are part of the process.

The mutuality, attunement, and empathy that emerge will help ensure that the therapeutic process is experienced in a fairly similar way by both therapist and patient. The fact that one person is intent on curing while the other is intent on being cured does not divide one experience from the other, because the process is interpersonal, between therapist and child. The experience is the same but may be defined in different words. Here are two parallel descriptions of the therapeutic process as given by the therapist and by the child patient. The therapist said:

> When I suggested that he was jealous of his brother and wished him harm, the patient became angry and raised his hand as if to strike me. Something seemed to stop him because his hand fell helplessly by his side and he murmured that since I was the therapist and supposedly knew what I was doing and got paid for what I was doing, that I must be right.

The child said:

> When he said to me that I was jealous of Ben, and wanted to hurt him, I felt myself becoming very angry and found my hand going up to hit him. There was something about him that seemed to stop me and I said that he must be right because he was a well-known and well-paid therapist and must certainly know what he was doing.

The therapeutic process, as experienced by both parties,

clearly involved an interpretation, a change in the patient's affect, an abortive attempt to retaliate physically, followed by a more or less conciliatory statement. Both therapist and child had segmented the process in roughly the same way and both added, in this particular case, nothing that was latent in the process. To a large extent, it is a one-sided statement since the therapist does not include any comment on the interior process set into action by the interpersonal process—the so-called countertransference process. The therapist might have reacted to the child's emotionally charged words such as "supposedly" and "well-paid." In the example given, two intrapsychic systems and one interpersonal system are brought together in time to generate a common process. Of course, all parts of it are not included in the description; another notable omission was the failure to mention the setting in which the process occurred.

Despite these omissions, it is still striking how much information (content) about therapy is conveyed in a few lines, though not enough to create a theory. To theorize about it, one would need to congeal the process and then examine it at a moment in time, abstracting its stationary, cross-sectional aspect. This would bring into focus something that one could label "structure." As Whitehead pointed out, it is difficult to understand how content is added to the flux of change. It is equally difficult to explain the emergence of a structure from a process. Nature discloses to scientific scrutiny merely process and change that fade sequentially into each other. They arise and then pass away. But something must remain, something must be enacted. If a pattern appears, something must be in the making. Looked at from this point of view, process begins to sound like something elusive, something open to common misconception and something that is difficult to capture realistically, without distorting its essence. These more or less philosophical concerns need emphasizing because the therapeutic process, like so many other clinical phenomena, might be taken for granted as a self-evident entity, which it is not.

Each natural pulsation of process forms a unit of historic fact, allowing us at best a tentative and intuitive selection of these facts from the flux of experience. But we choose in a highly selective manner since we experience far more than we can analyze. Without this constant selection procedure, intimations of process would be chaotic and confused.

We are all voyagers who, from time to time, make attempts to crystallize the moment in the "specious present." We try to seize the passing moment to construct artificially fabricated structures, seeking a moment of security in the midst of interminable change.

Most child therapists find a need to elaborate structure or to think structurally after a period of immersion in the ongoing therapeutic process. Our minds move along in a temporal relationship with the child patient, but when the session is over, and even before it is over, we begin to segment the interval, to create logical sequences, to describe "event systems," to structure the interactions, and begin to tell "stories" that become the content of our material. Following "recovery" from the therapeutic session, we can examine our notes, make sense of apparent nonsense and, from time to time, even allow our patients to share in this sense-making. Perhaps patients would benefit from being allowed to read the ongoing process notes kept by their therapist. They might then appreciate the professional work that goes into the reduction of an hour of non-directed outpouring into a page of coherent explanation.

To understand the therapeutic process, we need first to make it intelligible to ourselves and then to our patients. Here again, the philosopher Whitehead wrote, as if he were speaking to therapists, that "nothing is finally understood until its referenced process has been made evident."[1] We need, therefore, to make the latent process into manifest process, and the obscure process into evident process before we can memorialize the session in our records. Each encounter of the "selves-in-process" provides merely "snippets of understanding," but as our sense of structure grows and miniature theories are made, there is an increasing merger of the obscurely moving therapeutic stream with the growth of understanding. This entails an increasing appreciation of what went before, what appears to be happening now, and, dimly, what is portended in the still unexplored developments that are in the process of becoming.

Reference

1. Whitehead, A.N. *Modes of Thought*. New York: Macmillan, 1938.

2

THE HISTORY OF CHILD TREATMENT
IN WESTERN CULTURE

The history of treatment for mentally and emotionally disturbed children is the history of the culture and institutions of mankind. In all periods, it is obvious that two elements remain constant: The healer must believe in himself and his method, and the patient must have hope and faith in him. Throughout history both the theory and method of therapy reflect the changing social attitudes and beliefs of each era.

How the beliefs, attitudes, and actions of people are altered over the course of history is not well understood. It appears, however, that the various forms of child psychotherapy known today reflect attitudes toward children and the practice of child rearing—conceptions which have changed radically from those of antiquity.

ANCIENT THEORY AND PRACTICE

From antiquity to the fourth century A.D., infanticide of both legitimate and illegitimate children was common and accepted practice; it was not until 374 A.D. that a Roman law was passed which made it murder. Although slowly becoming less frequent during the Middle Ages, infanticide continued to be practiced until the nineteenth century. Any child with an abnormality or one who "cried too much or too little" could become a victim. Beating and abuse were common. Boys were castrated as preparation for the brothel or to have their testicles sold to make magic potions. Girls had little

9

value. The selling and sacrifice of children were also practiced.[1]

During this period, when little distinction was made between mind and body, disease was attributed to evil spirits.
Since healing was a part of religion, the priest and the physician were one. Incantations, amulets, and vile concoctions
were used to ward off demons. Faith in the method was
enhanced by elaborate ceremonies and magic. Although
Hippocrates of Cos (460-375 B.C.) had declared that insanity
was a disease of the brain, that idea was to be lost and not
revived for 12 centuries. With Christianity, the role of religion increased. Disease was often considered a punishment
for sin, inflicted by the Devil with God's permission. Confes-
sion and exorcism were the therapies.

Although children were not singled out for special ther-
apeutics, they were not completely unnoticed. Claudius Galen
(c. 129-199 A.D.), a Greek physician, believed that human
endowment was set at birth and that children display strongly
individual characteristics which could be modified only
within limits by training and education.[1]

THE MIDDLE AGES

Historians usually date the start of the Middle Ages as 476
A.D.—the fall of the Roman Empire. Zilboorg and Henry[2]
have claimed, however, that the Dark Ages for medicine began with the death of Galen. Although Galen had espoused
eclecticism and instructed others to think and look for themselves, for centuries his humoral theories and treatment were
blindly accepted. After his death, "knowledge, and with it
medicine, took refuge behind the walls of monasteries" (p.
204). Treatment of the mentally ill was eventually excluded
from medicine. Magic and demonology held sway.

With the spread of Christianity and the feudal system,
changes occurred in the attitudes toward children and child-

rearing practices. Commenting on the Middle Ages, Aries[3] writes that the "family . . . did not penetrate very far into human sensibility" (p. 411). Marriage was denigrated; wet nursing and apprenticeship loosened the emotional bonds between children and parents. The child had no special status; at about age seven, he* was "mixed with adults." Once parents had accepted the Church's teaching that the child had a soul, the killing of children was curtailed. "The only way they could escape the dangers of their own projections," according to DeMause,[1] "was by abandonment to the wet nurse, monastery, or nunnery, or by severe emotional abandonment at home" (p. 51). Originating in church doctrine and reinforced by the parents' projections was the belief that the child was born with sin and was therefore basically evil and needed beating. Contributing to the apparent lack of attachment to the child may have been the extremely high rate of infant and child mortality. Expecting the child to die, parents may have avoided attachment. However, Neugebauer[4] notes that, starting in the thirteenth century, the English government conducted mental status examinations using commonsense, naturalistic criteria of impairment, and etiological theories that relied on physiological and psychological notions of psychiatric illness.

THE RENAISSANCE

During the Renaissance (fourteenth to sixteenth centuries), although emotional acceptance of the child by the parents became more evident, he was still viewed suspiciously as the repository of dark forces demanding the strictest control. This attitude is reflected in the preoccupation of the period

---

*The traditional use of the pronoun *he* has not yet been superseded by a convenient, generally accepted pronoun that means either *he* or *she*. Therefore, the authors will continue to use *he* while acknowledging the inherent inequity of the traditional preference of the masculine pronoun.

with the child's feces, urine, and vomit: "No matter how placid and cooperative [a child] might appear, the excrement which was regularly washed out of him was regarded as the insulting message of an inner demon, indicating the 'bad humors' which lurked within" (p. 144).[5]

Writings of the time began to inveigh against some of the child-rearing practices. In 1540, Sebastian Oestereicher[5] spoke against the ancient and persistent custom of wet nursing:

> Those who abandon their infants, who thrust them from themselves and give them to others to bring up, cut and destroy the spiritual bond and the affection by which nature binds parents to their children. You can tell that an infant has been sent away to nurse by its eyes: for the strong affection for the mother is slowly and gradually extinguished and is centered alone upon her who nurses the child, which has no further inclination or love for the one who gave it birth (p. 137).

The practice of wet nursing also helped to perpetuate swaddling, another ancient and widespread custom. As Rousseau[6] was later to remark:

> These women [wet nurses] finding themselves mothers of strange children, lack the appeal of natural affection and are only concerned to save themselves bother. A child that has been left free needs constant watching; but if it is tightly bound it can be pitched into a corner where its cries will trouble no one (p. 16).

THE SEVENTEENTH AND EIGHTEENTH CENTURIES

In the seventeenth and eighteenth centuries, greater empathy developed for the child, who had come to be recognized as unique and separate from adults. Theologians, philosophers, educators, and physicians became more explicit in their advice to parents about child-rearing. Most of the advice was focused on preventing difficulties by the proper molding and training of the child, but there were excursions, as well, into the realm of treatment (for example, Locke's description of desensitizing childhood fears) (see below).

During the Renaissance, education gained vigor from the great works of Greece and Rome. Eventually, however, schools became mere pedantic mills for the teaching of Greek and Latin. Mainly for the wealthy, education was conducted by means of tutors. (Martin Luther had advocated "public schools" as early as 1524, but compulsory public education did not arrive until the late nineteenth century.)

Comenius[7] not only revolutionized the methods and curricula of education, but also led the way in altering adults' attitudes and behavior toward youngsters. Prevailing school practices aroused his sympathy for the children who

> were fisticuffed, beaten with pointers, canes and sticks on their cheeks, head, back and seat until they shed blood, and the majority of whom were full of bruises and scars, wales and calluses. . . . Only a small remnant persevered to the end (p. 24).

Comenius was a sharp observer of children. His book *School of Infancy*,[7] a guide to rearing children from conception to seven, shows that he recognized individual differences and maturational stages. He gave prime importance to the development of the soul (character); next came the body; then formal learning. He advocated leading the child to good habits and virtues by perpetual example, wise instruction, daily exercise, and gentle, regulated discipline. He recommended eating and sleeping according to nature's demands and the use of medicine only when necessary. The value of play was recognized as a means of learning and of mastery. Three centuries before Harry Stack Sullivan, moreover, he saw the importance of the "chum":

> Since one boy sharpens the genius of another boy more than anyone else can, boys should daily meet together and play and run about . . . Among them there is . . . love, candor, free discussion about anything that comes up. All these are missing when we older people deal with children. And this defect is a great obstacle to our free communication with them (p. 90).

Comenius espoused kindness and rational treatment of children, but cautioned against overindulgence. Good example and instruction were to prevent bad habits. If they did appear, they were to be nipped in the bud by rebukes, shame, and, as a last resort, "the rod or a slap, that the boy may recollect himself and become more attentive" (p. 102).

Comenius was a surprisingly "modern" figure. Many of the ideas first expressed by him were a foreshadowing of those which were to be fully developed in the years—indeed, centuries—after his death.

In 1692, John Locke wrote *Some Thoughts Concerning Education*.[8] In the form of a letter to a father, the book is mainly concerned with child-rearing practice, and the development of character.

One does not expect to find in Locke a detailed prototype of psychotherapy for troubled children. He wrote:

> The consideration I shall have of health shall be, not what a physician ought to do with a sick or crazy child but what the parents, without the help of physician, should do for the preservation and improvement of unhealthy, or at least not sickly, constitution in their children (p. 10).

Locke's interest, then, was in the area we would now call "orthopsychiatry" and guidance.

For Locke, the first consideration was health. He advised a rather modern diet—plain and simple, with little salt and preferably no sugar. The child should be hardened to the climate by the use of light, loose, clothing and exposure to the elements. Swaddling was condemned. His regimen for toilet training (perhaps the first treatise on the subject) included taking advantage of nature's urges after the child's breakfast.

Locke recognized the developmental stages of children and the individuality of each child. While considering the mind a *tabula rasa*, he also advocated studying the nature and aptitudes of the child. He advised observing the child during play to see the predominant passions and prevailing inclinations. Recognizing, as well, that each age showed certain characteristics, he recommended that "faults of their age rather than children themselves should be left only to time and imitation and riper years to cure" (p. 42).

Locke, although aware of "natural propensities" and different temperaments in children, emphasized the value of guidance from birth:

> I think I may say, that of all men we meet with, nine parts of ten are what they are, good or evil, useful or not, by their education . . . The little or almost insensible impressions on our tender infancies have very important and lasting consequences (p. 9)

Many of Locke's approaches, programs, and techniques have found their way into the techniques of psychotherapy and child-rearing practices of today.

He believed in the rationality of men. To achieve that state, however, the child had to learn to subjugate desire and passion to reason. He advised:

> And the great principles and foundation of all virtue and
> worth is placed in this: that a man is able to *deny himself* his
> own desires, cross his own inclinations and purely follow
> what reason directs best though the appetite leans the other
> way (p. 27).

Rousseau was later to criticize Locke severely for his alleg-
edly advising adults to reason with children. In some ways
this is a misreading of Locke, who had specifically said, "But
when I talk of reasoning, I do not intend any other but such
as is suited to the child's capacity and apprehension" (p. 64).
Rules were to be as few as possible. If chiding was necessary,
it was to be done in private and in sober, grave, and impas-
sioned words. Praise was to be given in public. Discipline was
to be relaxed as soon as age, discretion, and good behavior
allowed. None of the things to be learned, Locke believed,
should ever be made a burden to children or imposed as a
task.

In dealing with "those actions which tend to be vicious
habits," Locke held that "none should be forbidden children
till they are found guilty of them" (p. 67). In treating a child
who would not attend to his lessons, he advised careful observation to determine if the boy was listless only when he
approached his books. If he was vigorous at play in a favorite
game, then the game became the task until he was sick of it.
If the boy was listless and daydreaming at all times, then
further investigation was needed to find the cause. In that
vein Locke asked:

> Would you have him open his heart to you and ask your
> advice? You must begin to do so with him first, and by your
> carriage beget that confidence. Advise as an experienced
> friend and mingle nothing of command or authority (p.
> 82).

The cure of irrational fears by gradual exposure to the feared object or situation was described by Locke who cautioned not to "make too much haste, nor attempt this cure too early, lest you increase the mischief instead of remedying it" (p. 98). In describing the process or method, he gave the following example:

> Your child shrieks and runs away at the site of a frog, let another catch it and lay it down a good distance from him: at first accustom him to look upon it; when he can do that, then to come nearer to it and see it leap without emotion; then to touch it lightly, when it is held in another's hand; and so on, till he can come to handle it as confidently as a butterfly or a sparrow. By the same way any other vain terrors may be reassured; if care be taken, that you go not too fast, and push not the child on to a new degree of assurance till he be thoroughly confirmed in the former (p. 99).

Jean-Jacques Rousseau's *Emile*,[9] published in 1762, echoed many of Locke's ideas and methods, despite Rousseau's specific disagreements with Locke in certain areas of philosophy and theory. The gap between the two thinkers narrows when their texts are studied in their totality.

Rousseau (1712-1778) emphasized the innate goodness and natural development of the child which would flower if not contaminated by society and the pedagogy of the time. In theory, he was thus somewhat more suspicious than was Locke about the exercise of adult control in shaping the behavior of children. Locke would have the father's benign authority established from infancy, whereas Rousseau advised his readers,

> Do not let [the child] imagine that you claim any authority over him. Let him only know that he is weak and you are strong, and that therefore he is at your mercy (p. 55).

(Unlike Comenius, whose remarks had been primarily directed at the mother, both Locke and Rousseau were addressing their advice to the father.) Rousseau went so far as to state that he would give no verbal lessons, but simply allow the child to learn by experience and necessity and without resort to punishment. His actual methods, however, often belie these claims. In practice, he was not dissimilar to Locke.

Like Locke, Rousseau also used deconditioning techniques. In dealing with fear of the dark, for example, Rousseau advocated getting the child to become preoccupied with pleasurable games in the dark. He would also give the child a task to do in hopes that the wish for approval or another emotion would prove greater than the fear (which, as we would say now, could ultimately be "extinguished").

Another influence on Rousseau, according to Seguin,[10] was Jacob Rodriguez Péreire (1715-1780), who had a school for deaf mutes. Péreire had at first used a manual alphabet described in 1620 by the Spaniard, Juan Pablo Bonnet. Adding 40-odd signs of his own and also using pantomime, he was able to communicate with his patients. He taught them that each sound produced by speech had a unique vibration which could be detected by the skin; they eventually learned to reproduce the vibration with their vocal apparatus.

Since Rousseau lived near Péreire, the two visited frequently. Seguin put it bluntly:

> The book *Emile* is full of experiments upon physiological teaching which could only have originated in the school for deaf mutes; so identical are the theories of the book with the practice of Péreire (p. 25).

Actually, many of Rousseau's ideas had been expressed by others before *Emile* was published. In setting forth the claim that all knowledge and ideas are acquired through the experience of the physical senses—as opposed to Descartes and his doctrine of innate ideas—Rousseau was following in the steps of Comenius and Locke. Rousseau's genius lay in his ability to convince others.[11]

THE NINETEENTH CENTURY

The nineteenth century gave rise to many of the movements and theories that, with some allowances for changing terminology, are easily recognizable as the direct antecedents of contemporary child-rearing practices and psychotherapeutic techniques. The successful application of scientific methods to the training of the mentally retarded and other deviant children both reflected and furthered an atmosphere of therapeutic optimism and social consciousness.

Whatever the origin of the idea that all knowledge is acquired through the senses, the concept became the core principle of educators such as Friedrich Froebel (1782-1852) and Johann Heinrich Pestalozzi (1746-1827). For the treatment of deviant children, it became the basis for the methods used by a number of humane and innovative therapists in the nineteenth century who sought to reach the mind and intellect by the training and stimulation of the body and the physiological development of the senses.

The training of the retarded

Jean-Marc-Gaspard Itard (1775-1848), the first to apply to other deviant groups the "physiological" techniques with the deaf mutes developed by Péreire, is best remembered for his remarkable work, *The Wild Boy of Aveyron*.[12]

In 1800, Itard began the treatment of a feral child at the institution for the deaf and mute where the 12-year-old boy had been placed not long after he had been discovered by hunters. The venerable Philippe Pinel, who had examined the youngster, considered him to be an idiot. Itard at first disagreed. He thought that "Victor" had become abnormal because of deprivation and isolation from society.

After five years of steady and inventive work, Itard regarded his treatment efforts as a failure because the boy had not acquired speech. Itard's contemporaries, to the contrary, were astounded by Victor's progress, that "he lived like a human being; clean, affectionate, even able to read a few words and to understand much of what was said to him" (p. xi). Victor died in 1827 at the age of 40; Itard died ten years later. Although he had gained considerable fame throughout Europe for his work with the Wild Boy, he never attempted to treat another child as severely handicapped as Victor.

Edouard Seguin (1812-1880), Itard's pupil, was undaunted by his teacher's discouragement. At the Bicêtre, he continued his work with mentally retarded children. Apparently a number of his young charges were, in fact, psychotic or suffering from severe learning disabilities. Seguin recognized that they were by no means congenital idiots, but took them on anyway. As he said, they had no other place to go.

In 1846, he published the fruit of his 10 years' experience in *Traitement Moral, Hygiène et Éducation des Idiots. . . .*[13] Shortly thereafter he was invited to America, where he was instrumental in spreading his methods and establishing institutions for the mentally retarded. In 1866, Seguin's *Idiocy and Its Treatment By the Physiological Method* was published in English.[14]

In addition to describing the physiological training of the senses, Seguin's books also dealt with "Moral treatment," an approach espoused by Pinel, among others—essentially what one knows today as milieu and psychological therapy.

Seguin saw his moral treatment as devoted to the "socialization" of the idiot—an unremitting, devoted coaxing of the isolated child into society. He said:

> For our pupils, science, literature, art, education, medicine, philosophy, each may do something; but love alone can socialize them; those alone who love them are their true rescuers (p. 245).

Physical punishment was never used. Benign coercion, however, was thought to be necessary at the onset of treatment. Initially, this might be on a one-to-one basis; thereafter the influence on the patient might be peer group pressure. Seguin was quite willing to use other patients as therapists, believing that "very many things are taught from child to child that we could not at all, or not so well, inculcate ourselves" (p. 219). Recognizing the gifts of certain child care workers, he remarked:

> Though generally quite illiterate, some of these attendants soon develop . . . moral powers which many educated persons cannot equal because sociability, not learning gives it; and though this power is susceptible of being educated . . . it looks more like a gift than an intellectual faculty (p. 219).

Seguin's work was carried on by Felix Voisin (1794-1872), a colleague at the Bicêtre, who later organized a service for "idiot" children in another public hospital and eventually helped found his own private institution, the Orthophrenic Establishment at Vanvres, near Paris.

Voisin, seeking to modify treatment to suit the individual patient, developed a classification scheme which comprised four categories, including children born to mentally ill patients, whom he recognized as "high risk."[15]

The attitudes and training techniques of Itard, Seguin, and Voisin continue to be echoed in modern programs for the mentally retarded, the psychotic youngster, and those with crippling learning disabilities. In many respects, the methods and the values they embody were the forerunners of a modern, behaviorally oriented therapy. The educator Maria Montessori (1870-1952), who had begun her medical career working with mentally retarded children, was to be greatly influenced by the writings of those who, a century before, had pioneered in the education of the defective youngster.

Building on the work of others, the proponents of physiologic training contributed to the growing change in attitudes toward children in the nineteenth century. They promoted the idea that children were different from adults and had unique problems related to distinct developmental stages. They recognized the deleterious effects of "bad education" and poor environment as well as heredity. These views were given great impetus when Charles Darwin (1809-1882) published *The Origin of Species* in 1859, a work which set others to thinking in terms of genetics, of development and evolving functions, and the interrelationship between the individual and the environment. In addition, Darwin later set off a rash of observations on infants and children when, in 1877, he published his notes—written originally some 30 years before—of his own son's growth and development.[16]

Hypnosis and the origins of dynamic psychiatry

A strong factor in the eventual emergence of dynamic psychiatry was the popular and scientific interest in hypnotism throughout the hundred years preceding Freud's birth.[17]

"Animal magnetism," a concept central to the thought of Franz Anton Mesmer, a Viennese physician (1734-1815), derived from a belief in the existence of a "subtle physical field," the unequal distribution of which is the source of human disease. His therapy, therefore, involved a variety of techniques—magnets, rods, mirrors, and magnetized trees—as well as his own curative touch, having to do with an infusion of fluid, which restored the suffering patient's equilibrium. Mesmer and his followers conceived of healing as occurring through crises; symptoms were to be produced in the somnambulant state and then controlled by the therapist.

In later developments of "mesmerism" (or "hypnotism," as James Braid labeled it in 1843), the "fluid" theory was abandoned and the search for more scientifically acceptable explanations of the phenomenon began. The psychological dimension was noted by Amand-Marie-Joseph de Chastenet, Marquis de Puységeur (1751-1825), a disciple of Mesmer in the 1780s, who realized that the rapport between therapist and patient was essential to the process. Once a strong rapport was established, the will of the therapist could produce an "artificial somnambulism" during which the patient would perform various acts or be relieved of symptoms.

Although appearing alert and awake, the individual would, in fact, be amnesic for the experience. James Braid (1795-1860), a Manchester surgeon who had originally sought a physiological explanation for the phenomenon, also came to sense intuitively that unconscious psychological processes were at work in hypnotism.

By 1860, when Auguste Ambroise Liébeault (1823-1904), a country doctor near Nancy, began to study and practice the method, hypnotism had fallen into general disrepute. His work was dismissed as that of a quack until 1882, when Hippolyte Bernheim (1840-1919), a professor of internal medicine at the new university in Nancy, began to use Liébeault's techniques therapeutically and revealed them to the world. Bernheim believed that hypnosis was produced by suggestion and that everyone was suggestible to a certain degree. He later found that he could obtain good results by using suggestion even in the waking state, a method he termed "psychotherapeutics." Like Liébeault, Bernheim treated all sorts of diseases with suggestion—organic or functional—and patients of all ages—children, as well as adults. By alleviating pain or removing inhibitions, Bernheim thought, the body's natural processes would be left free to work the cure.

Bernheim's stand concerning hypnosis contrasted sharply with that of Jean-Martin Charcot (1835-1893) of the Salpêtrière. As the preeminent neurologist of his day, he considered the hypnotic state a pathological condition found only in hysterics. As the debate waged on, the different neuroses came to be recognized once again as respectable subjects for medical study. In the following years, the interest in hypnotism—having gained scientific stature—was to give rise to the development of a system of dynamic psychopathology.

In 1886, Pierre Janet (1859-1947),[18] who had already set forth his theories of "dissociation" and "subconscious fixed ideas," adopted hypnosis as a technique for recovering a dissociated traumatic memory. Suggestion was also used by Janet to "strengthen the resources of psychically impoverished patients."

In the early 1880s, Sigmund Freud (1856-1939), who had worked with both Charcot and Bernheim, became interested in Joseph Breuer's cathartic method. In treating "Anna O." with hypnosis, Breuer had found that it was not sufficient to "recall the circumstances under which the symptoms had appeared the first time" (p. 30).[18] Anna "told Breuer, in reverse chronological order, each appearance of a given symptom with exact dates, until she reached the original manifestation and initial event, and then the symptom disappeared" (p. 30).[18]

In hypnosis, Breuer and Janet had discovered, a painful memory—accompanied by strong emotion—could be relieved by a catharsis that had therapeutic value. (Although the concept of catharsis goes back to Aristotle and his theories of the drama, its use in psychotherapy and hypnotherapy is relatively recent.) It was Freud's eventual conclusion, however, that the "dissociation" proposed by Janet was not just because of the inherent weakness of the patient, but because impulses had been purposely "pushed" from awareness, or "repressed" to protect the individual. When his patient, Elisabeth von R., taught him the value of "free association," Freud had the rudiments of a new theory *and* a new therapeutic method, and he abandoned hypnosis.

While Freud was to make the role of the therapist central to his psychoanalytic work, Emile Coué (1857-1926)—another of Bernheim's students—developed a treatment method which he claimed was not dependent on the mediation of another person. In his clinic at Nancy, which contained a children's section, Coué used the technique of "induced autosuggestion."

Neuroses, he held, were thoughts and ideas which had become realities in the unconscious by means of "spontaneous autosuggestion." To implant ideas of health into the unconscious and have them accepted, according to Coué, no effort of will was to be used. The more the patient tried to conquer his illness, drug-taking, or fears, the more the idea of the affliction would be implanted, become an obsession, and be carried out as real by the unconscious. Autosuggestion, he believed, succeeded by avoiding conflict and implanting positive thoughts.

Coué's technique, invented before the turn of the century, gained considerable vogue for a brief period after the publication of his *Self Mastery Through Conscious Autosuggestion*[19] in 1922. In this book, he advised the patient to approach his or her unconscious when it was most accessible, either when the patient was falling asleep or upon awakening. Assuming a comfortable position—muscles relaxed and eyes closed—the patient would naturally fall into a state of semiconsciousness like daydreaming. The patient was then to repeat 20 times, "Every day, in every way, I am getting better and better." As the patient repeated the process day after day. Coué reasoned, the autosuggestion became stronger and the unconscious would accept as reality the new idea of health.

Prior to 1921, the children's department of the Nancy

Clinic was managed by Mlle. Kauffmant, a devoted disciple of Coué.[20]

> In a large room decorated with bright pictures and equipped with toys, the mothers and their sick children would form a wide circle around Mlle. Kauffmant. She would take each child on her lap in turn and in a crooning tone mingled with endearing phrases, she would suggest that no matter what the trouble was, organic, functional, or behavioral, it was getting better. For about ten minutes she gave her undivided attention to each child while the mothers and other children listened. As she talked, she would stroke and caress the child, varying her talk and manipulations depending on the child's age and problem (p. 36).

If the child was old enough to talk, of course, he or she was required to go through the "day by day, in every way" litany morning and night.

The mother was encouraged "to set an example of cheerfulness and confidence" so that the malady was alluded to only in terms of encouragement and recovery. At night, the mother was to whisper good suggestions into the sleeping child's ear. For boys after the age of seven or eight, the father was to take over. If possible, both the parents and the therapist were to avoid all mention of the ailment or difficulty. The attention of the child was to be directed not so much toward getting rid of "wrong" conditions, but toward replacing them by cultivating the opposite "right" ones.

Whether it was by autosuggestion, suggestion, faith, or their loving and charismatic personalities, there is no doubt that Coué and his disciples helped or cured many patients.

The "imposition" of the hypnotist on patient which Coué had rejected was even more odious for Paul Dubois (1848-1918), professor of psychotherapy at the University of Bern. Admitting that Bernheim and Janet had done brilliant work,

Dubois found their use of authority and suggestion none-theless repugnant.

Every illness, according to Dubois, has a mental represen-tation. Organic illness may be exacerbated by false ideas; functional nervous diseases are caused by mental represen-tations. To alleviate or cure the illness, the false beliefs and opinions must be replaced by correct ones. The technique he advocated was called "The Method of Persuasion," an attempt to educate or reeducate the patient by using proofs, demonstrations, and "sentimental logic" (heart-to-heart talks). Dubois believed the therapist should have daily sessions with the patient and should be sincere, honest, and caring.

"The Method of Persuasion" and its originator gained con-siderable fame following the publication of Dubois's book in 1905.[21] In 1909, he outlined his psychotherapeutic technique in a series of articles published in the United States. By that time, however, there were other developments within this country and abroad which were to put their stamp on the practices of child-rearing and child therapy in the twentieth century, later dubbed "The Century of the Child."[22]

THE TWENTIETH CENTURY

Some of the developments which presaged important aspects of what we know today as therapy with children are traced in the following pages but only to 1940. Moreover, only a few topics from among the many have been selected: play therapy, the child psychiatry and guidance clinics, the hos-pital and residential treatment centers for children and ad-olescents, behavior therapy, and child psychopharmacology.

Play therapy

"One of the great ironies in the history of psychoanalysis," Kern[23] has written, "is that Freud, who laid the foundation

for twentieth-century child psychiatry never personally analyzed a child" (p. 365). The case of "Little Hans" permitted
Freud[24] to confirm certain ideas about the early origins of
neuroses that until then he had only been able to abstract
from the retrospection of his adult patients. The work with
Little Hans, however, was almost exclusively at the hands of
his father, Max Graf, a Viennese musicologist and critic who
was an early admirer of Freud and a member of his weekly
discussion group.

The details of the four-month "analysis" of Little Hans are
familiar. Although the form of therapeutic intervention with
the boy was generally just conversation between father and
son, Graf did note that the content of the child's play seemed
related to his fears.

Freud thought the work with Little Hans was a virtually
unique instance in which the technical problems of dealing
with a child were overcome by the boy's special rapport with
the father and the latter's excellent knowledge of psychoanalysis. It remained, therefore, for Freud's followers to develop methods for treating child patients in the consultation
room.

The earliest description of the direct treatment of children
by a psychoanalyst was published in 1921 by Hermine von
Hug-Hellmuth.[25] She used toys with children seven or
younger, but considered play techniques helpful even with
older children as a means of eliciting verbal material for
analysis. Von Hug-Hellmuth did not work with patients
younger than six, however, nor did she develop specific techniques for child psychoanalysis. The practice of psychoanalysis with children was shaped most clearly by two other
women—Melanie Klein (1882-1960) and Anna Freud (1895-
)—both of whom began their careers in Europe and later
moved to Great Britain.

Klein's method of "play analysis" (outlined in *Psychoanalysis
of Children* published in 1932)[26] was developed over a long

career of direct work with children, beginning with the analysis of a five-year-old boy in his own home. Convinced that the nature of the play with the generous variety of toys she made available to her patients was essentially similar to the free association of the adult analysand, Klein made "depth" interpretations of the play, including references to the transference. Early intervention of this kind, she believed, reduced the child's intitial anxiety. Her observations of children also led Klein to some theoretical differences with Sigmund Freud; she held, for example, that the superego begins to develop in early infancy and that the Oedipus complex appears in some forms much before the fourth or fifth year of life. Although aware of the differences between child and adult patients, Klein, even with children, tried to work along classical psychoanalytic lines. The emphasis, therefore, was placed on the exclusivity of the relationship between the child patient and the analyst; there was a minimum of contact with parents and teachers.

Anna Freud, on the other hand, assumed that the differences between children and grown-ups necessitated some rather drastic adaptations of technique when working with young analysands. Rather than moving in quickly with interpretations, she posited the value of a "preparatory phase" in which the child—who, after all, comes to therapy through no choice of his or her own—is slowly brought to feel the necd for treatment and grows to like and be dependent upon the therapist. The work of treatment cannot, she posited, use the transference neurosis because children, still under the influence of their real parents, do not develop transferences in a manner analogous to adults. Moreover, one must reckon with the immaturity of the superego in younger children. Therefore, the analyst assumed a certain *educative* function—along with that of making the unconscious conscious—and had, in some cases, to be willing to intervene in the outside world on behalf of the patient.

The child analyst who followed Freudian tenets tended to be relatively less active than the Kleinian and would supply fewer toys with which the child was to play. Interpretations, as well, would be proffered much more cautiously. Anna Freud's first discussions of the techniques of child psychotherapy and psychoanalysis are contained in an early work, published in 1928, *Introduction to the Technique of Child Analysis.*[27]

Throughout the 1930s, orthodox child psychoanalytic practices of both the Freudian and Kleinian schools were adapted to the clinical necessities of brief and less intensive intervention with children.

In 1937, David M. Levy published a book on sibling rivalry in which he included a description of a treatment and research method he called "structured play therapy."[28] In essence, the technique required the therapist to set up for the child a play situation which deliberately replicated an area of real-life conflict for the youngster. Where sibling rivalry was the issue, for example, the child was exposed to doll play in which a mother doll was nursing the baby while the older brother or sister watched.

Jacob Conn[29] and Joseph Solomon[30] extended some of Levy's procedures into techniques variously named "active" or "situational" play therapy. Dolls and props were set up in the playroom in a manner which was to suggest to the child the very life-situation with which he or she was struggling (the therapist, of course, would know of this beforehand). One of the dolls—whether or not the youngster was conscious of the fact—represented the patient. In the relationship with the therapist, the child was led to achieve insight into the problem and to discover better ways of handling the difficulty.

It is of interest that the child's "understanding" and mastery came to be deemphasized in a later transformation of the "structured" play technique called by David Levy "release therapy."[31] Under certain conditions—with a very young child, for example, and in dealing with a problem which was fairly circumscribed and no longer current—Levy relied on structured play chiefly for purposes of abreaction ("acting out").

While orthodox psychoanalysis was infiltrating many of the child guidance and psychiatric clinics in the persons of European refugees to North America, the influence of a "schismatic," Otto Rank, was also being felt. Rank had broken with Freud in the late 1920s. His disciple, Jessie Taft, a psychologist who was later to teach in the School of Social Work of the University of Pennsylvania, developed a method of working with children which was termed "relationship therapy."

For Taft, the major emphasis is on the curative effects of the emotional rapport between patient and therapist in an atmosphere of great acceptance, focus upon the "here and now," and quiet insistence upon the child's exercising his or her freedom of action and choice. Her textbook, *The Dynamics of Therapy in a Controlled Relationship*, published in 1933, was the first of its kind to be written by an American;[32] with its philosophical and humanitarian cast, it remains fascinating and instructive reading. (The "controlled relationship" in the title refers to the strictures of time rather than the domination of the psychotherapist.) Taft's colleague in the Philadelphia Child Guidance Clinic, Frederick Allen,[33] was to continue to develop the ideas of "relationship therapy" and to influence the eventual emergence in the 1940s and early 1950s, of the theory of "non-directive" play therapy articulated by Virginia Axline[34] and Elaine Dorfman,[35] two students of Carl Rogers.

The child clinics

In the wider sense, "treatment" does not refer only to the specific moves and strategies of a single therapist. It also includes the institutional setting and philosophy which influ-

ences the conditions under which children are seen. Some
reference must therefore be made to the "clinic," a phenomenon of the twentieth century which for a long period was
almost synonymous with outpatient psychological and psychiatric services for children in this country.

The Psychological Clinic at the University of Pennsylvania,
established in 1893 by the psychologist Lightner Witmer, is
generally considered to be the very first institution of this
type. Witmer's clinic, which continued in operation until 1961
and was an important training center, devoted much of its
early efforts to tutoring children with learning problems and
collaborating with the parents, schools, and other social agencies. (Play therapy was introduced into the Clinic only after
World War II.)[36]

Although Witmer had relatively little influence on the development of the child guidance movement (he identified
himself with the rather unimaginative schemas of Wilhelm
Wundt and Emil Kraepelin and apparently did not think
much of psychodynamic formulations), he is a figure of considerable historical interest.[37] The journal which he founded
in 1907, *The Psychological Clinic*, was a clearinghouse for research and a major vehicle for interdisciplinary communication about children until it ceased publication in 1935.
Witmer, furthermore, was one of the first clinicians to attempt to differentiate between childhood psychosis and mental deficiency.[38] He was not only an astute and experienced
observer of children but also employed his own brand of
psychoeducational therapy as a means for ongoing differ-
ential diagnosis.

Along with the more familiar problems one would expect
to find in the school system, Witmer also dealt successfully
with severely handicapped youngsters. "P.", a child whose
treatment by a teacher in the 1890s was supervised by Witmer,[39] was apparently a victim of early infantile autism ("his
mental defects being the result of severe convulsions while

teething" (p. 466) dates the onset of the symptoms). Miss Marvin, P.'s teacher, worked with the child for four years—five days a week, three hours a day! After first "shaping" the attention of the child (he was then seven years of age), she proceeded to train P.'s sensory modalities. Building upon many of the skills that P. already had (but was using bizarrely), Miss Marvin helped the child develop the rudiments of speech and appropriate social habits. P. apparently learned to speak normally. By the time treatment had ended, moreover, this autistic child "could write all his alphabet and several words . . . could add and subtract to six; could sing about twelve songs with piano accompaniment, and could read very nicely" (p. 470).

Witmer's clinic was the prototype after which, in 1909, William Healy fashioned the psychiatric service for children associated with the Juvenile Court of Chicago. Healy, who had been recommended to the post by his former teacher, Adolf Meyer, came uniquely prepared. An associate professor of nervous and mental diseases at Chicago Polyclinic for the previous 13 years, he received his early training not only with Meyer but also with G. Stanley Hall and William James.

At the outset, the clinic for children was more properly a delinquency study financed single-handedly by Mrs. Ethel S. Dummer, a remarkable woman who had fought for Healy's appointment and his control over the project.

During Healy's tenure, he introduced the use of Binet's tests into the evaluation, established the team concept in child guidance (the "holy trinity" of physician, psychologist, and social worker, as Leo Kanner once put it), and welcomed psychologic and "dynamic" thinking in the assessment and treatment of children. Another of Healy's major contributions was his focus on the individual child through detailed and firsthand case study and observation.

In 1916, a year after the publication of his great work, *The Individual Delinquent*,[40] Healy—disappointed because the facilities for the treatment of delinquents in Chicago were few and apparently not forthcoming—left to become head of the Judge Baker Foundation in Boston. The clinic in Chicago, under the direction of Herman Adler, achieved state support in 1920 and became the Institute of Juvenile Research.

The experience with children with school problems (Witmer) and those who were in trouble with the law (Healy) prepared the groundwork for the rise and growth of the child guidance movement. Further impetus came in 1921, when the Commonwealth Fund issued a report advocating the establishment of a number of demonstration child guidance clinics to be associated exclusively with juvenile courts. From 1922 to 1927, a number of clinics were founded throughout the country under the aegis of the Fund. Interestingly, the clinics soon tended to shift their caseloads away from court referrals in the direction of treating children brought in by parents or sent by schools and other community agencies.[41] Several of the clinics continued to function with community support after the grant period ended.

The Commonwealth Fund's interest and financial resources helped establish a network of clinics from which issued important child research and a number of individuals who played preeminent roles in American child psychiatry.

The residential treatment center and psychiatric hospital for children.

The emergence of special 24-hour-a-day treatment facilities for the emotionally disturbed youngster is perhaps as complicated a tale as any we have so far attempted. The way was prepared by a long and meandering series of experiments in dealing with the juvenile delinquent, the abandoned child, and the severely handicapped.[42]

Separate institutions for delinquent youth have a long history, going back as far as the end of the seventeenth century in Germany. It was not until 1825, however, that the first juvenile penal institution was established in the United States, when the New York House of Refuge, operated by a private charitable group, opened its doors to six children. More than 20 years passed before the first publicly supported reformatory for delinquents was set up by the Commonwealth of Massachusetts in Westborough.

The goal of these "reformatories" was, as their name implied, to change the criminal habits of the young according to the best penological principles of the day. The ideals to which wardens subscribed, however, were rarely realized. Rather than providing their charges with individualized programs, educational opportunities, and incentives for positive change, the institutions—flooded with inmates—usually operated with only the goal of regimentation and control. The very design of the adult penitentiaries—the enforced silence between prisoners and the horrendous isolation to which they were subjected (ostensibly to provide time for reflection and contrition)—was all too often copied in the institutions for the delinquent child.

In the nineteenth century, both public and private agencies became interested in children who, unlike the delinquent, could not be held responsible for their plight. The Civil War and the steadily growing numbers of immigrants into the country filled the cities with orphans and other children who, for all practical purposes, were abandoned to the streets. Again, the very names of the institutions founded to deal with these youngsters show the intent of the organizers. In 1853, for example, the Northern Home for Friendless Children was opened in Philadelphia. Two years later, the Children's Village was established in Dobbs Ferry, New York, simply to house youngsters who had no place to live. Another group of unfortunate children singled out for care were the retarded. As has been previously described, Edouard Seguin's popularity in the United States around the middle of the nineteenth century eventuated in the development of a number of publicly financed "schools" for the mentally defective. (There was later to be a backlash of disappointment at the supposed failure of Seguin's methods. The institution for idiots established in 1894 in Rome, New York, for instance, was tellingly called the "State Custodial Asylum.")

As children in their numbers pressed themselves upon the attention of society, public opinion slowly began to differentiate between them and adults. In Massachusetts, for example, special court hearings for juveniles were instituted in 1870; the first juvenile court came into existence in 1890 (in South Australia). In 1872, again in Massachusetts, poor children were required by law to be separated from grown-ups in the state almshouses.

Along with the legal and social differentiation of children from adults came the beginning of psychiatric awareness that the young are victims of their own particular versions of mental illness. In 1867, Henry Maudsley's textbook, *The Physiology and Pathology of the Mind*,[43] contained a small chapter on "the insanity of early life." Twenty years later, Emminghaus produced an entire monograph devoted to the nervous and mental diseases of childhood.[44]

In the first four decades of the twentieth century, a number of institutions which had been originally founded as orphanages or reformatories evolved into residential treatment centers. Among these were the Parsons Child and Family Center in Albany, New York, begun in 1829 as a privately sponsored orphan asylum, and Hawthorne-Cedar Knolls, originally established in 1906 by the Jewish Protecting and Aid Society of New York as a model reformatory built on the cottage plan first introduced in France and Great Britain. As the agency grew more accepting of psychiatric ideas and the mental health professions seemed to have more to offer, the staff came also to include psychologists, psychiatrists, and social workers. Following the lead of the neighboring Pleasantville Cottage School, Hawthorne included a child guidance clinic on the premises in 1935. In 1937, finally, it became the institution's policy that each and every child was to receive psychotherapy in line with an individualized treatment plan. Over the course of 30 years, the reformatory had become a treatment facility. The stories of Bellefaire (founded in 1868 as the Cleveland Jewish Orphan Home), the Berkshire Farm Center and Services for Youth, and the Ryther Child Center in Seattle are not dissimilar.

Psychiatric hospital facilities for children were originally founded to deal with the large number of post-encephalitic children left in need of special care by the influenza epidemic that swept this country after World War I.[45] In 1920 and 1921, the first state psychiatric facilities for youngsters were established in Bellevue and Kings Park State Hospital. The Southard School in Topeka (founded in 1926) and the Emma Pendleton Bradley Home in Providence (which came into existence in 1931) originally catered, in the main, to children who were clearly brain-injured (post-encephalitic, convulsive, cerebrospastic). Only later did they reorganize themselves as hospitals for youngsters with severe emotional and behavior problems. It was not until 1933, moreover, that Howard Potter[46] documented the tragic fact that large numbers of schizophrenic children were mistakenly being placed and left untreated in institutions for the mentally deficient.

Behavior therapy

Beginning in the late 1950s and continuing to the present, there has been an outpouring of books and articles which seek to apply the principles of learning to the solution of clinical problems. Behavior modification has strong historic ties to academic psychology and to the tradition of research on animal learning that was particularly characteristic of American experimental psychology since the time of E. L.

Thorndike. It is therefore not surprising that the first ad-
herents and practitioners of behavior modification were
mainly psychologists and that the child in school, with learning and/or behavior problems, remained a focus of interest
for them. More recently, child psychiatrists and social workers have also been enlisted in the ranks of those whose treatment techniques are heavily influenced by learning theory.

The immediate ancestor of behavior therapy was John B.
Watson (1878-1958), the self-proclaimed "behaviorist." His
book, *Psychology from the Point of View of a Behaviorist*,[47] published in 1919, articulated the revolt against the "introspectionism" of German psychology and offered in its stead a
model of human behavior based on the work of Ivan Pavlov
and V. M. Bekhterev with the "conditioned reflex." For at
least 20 years, Watson's writings exerted enormous influence
on child-rearing and stamped the constraints of strict em-
piricism on research regarding human learning.[48]

Two case histories of children are important in the history
of behaviorism. In 1921, Watson published the case of "Albert," an 11-month-old child, in whom a fear response to a
white rat had been conditioned by the experimenter making
a sudden loud sound whenever Albert reached for the animal. The response of frightened withdrawal soon generalized
to a white rabbit, other furry things, and even to a Santa
Claus mask.[49] Mary Cover Jones, a graduate student at Columbia was inspired by Watson to undertake a project in which
a three-year-old boy, Peter, who was already afraid of ani-
mals, was eventually freed of his phobia by a systematic "extinction" procedure and by "modeling"[50] (shades of Locke)!

Another important study which successfully applied learning principles to a clinical problem was that of O. Hobart
Mowrer and his wife, who treated a series of 30 enuretic
children at the New Haven Children's Community Center,
a residential facility.[51] The Mowrers improved upon a bell-
and-pad device which had long been available for use in toilet

training. The children were then taught to become sensitized to the internal cues for bladder fullness. There was 100 percent success in the training, no symptom substitution, and a general post-treatment improvement in adjustment.

The work of Watson and the Mowrers illustrates the first behavioral approach to learning—classical conditioning. Other learning approaches (operant or Skinnerian learning, modeling, and social learning) have been equally powerful in generating strategies for ameliorating difficulties with children in settings which range from the home and classroom to hospitals and residential treatment centers. Indeed, the operant model has produced a large number of studies in which parents have been taught procedures for dealing with disruptive and problem behavior in their own children.

Psychopharmacology

Among the near-revolutions in contemporary child psychiatry is that of the addition of psychopharmacologic agents to the treatment repertoire. Relative to the amount of time, energy, and publications devoted to drug treatment of adult psychopathology, psychopharmacologic research with children has been severely limited. The history of psychopharmacology shows quite clearly that preadolescents have been the last age group to which innovations of drug therapy have been applied.

In searching for the history of child psychopharmacologic treatment, one must acknowledge that the favorite adult nostrums of physicians in the nineteenth century also came to be used with younger patients. A table (taken from Weiner and Jaffe's recent book[52]) drives home the point that before the fourth decade of the twentieth century there was almost no childhood psychopharmacology deserving of the name (see Table 1).

The population of children at whom most of the recent

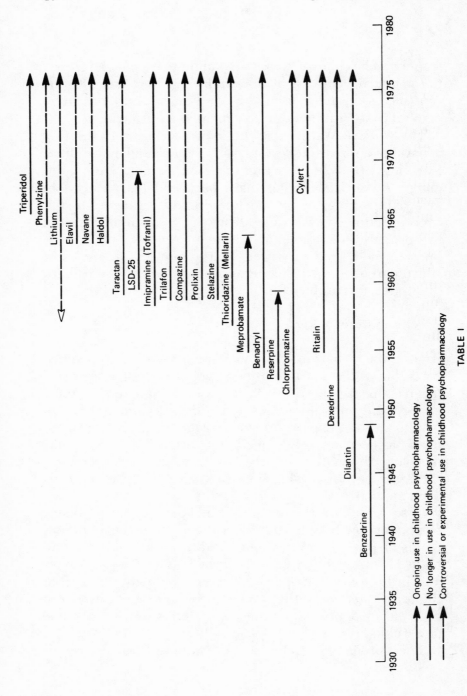

TABLE I

psychopharmacologic research has been directed is that characterized as minimal brain damage (MBD) or "hyperactive," who have been found to respond beneficially to stimulants. The roots of this research lie in the work of Bradley and his colleagues[53,54] at the Emma Pendleton Bradley Home, who investigated the effects of amphetamine (Benzedrine) on a number of children varying in age from five to 14 years, running the whole gamut of childhood psychopathology (learning problems, schizoid withdrawal, and epilepsy). Although Bradley found their responses varied, he was nonetheless impressed with some rapid and marked improvements in about half of the children.

At about the same time, Molitch and his colleagues[55,56] found that doses of Benzedrine increased verbal IQs in a sample of children and adolescents committed to the New Jersey State Home for Boys. Molitch and Poliakoff[57] also administered the drug to a number of severely enuretic children at the Home and showed that the drug was quite effective in helping lessen the symptoms or completely remit them.

Into the early 1940s, Benzedrine continued to be almost the only drug whose effects were studied in a population of child patients. The work of Lauretta Bender[58] on the children's ward at Bellevue Hospital led her to distinguish among diagnostic groups in their response to the drug. Schizophrenic youngsters and those with organic brain disease, for example, were found to either show no response to the medication or, indeed, to show exacerbation of symptoms.

CONCLUSION

The story of methods for treating the deviant child is, as we have said at the outset, virtually synonymous with the chronicle of humankind's attempt to understand itself and its environment. It is the story of the spirit of a time and of the

men and women who were a product of it. Some remained
bound and clung to old and current customs, but a few with
genius and courage prompted the evolution of new techniques.

To write the final history of these endeavors so that "truth"
is assured is impossible. The mass of data is indigestible and
eludes integration.

The limits of space have prevented us from showing in
more detail how child therapy has always been a creature of
its times—responding to and influencing trends of popular
belief, public policy, the atmosphere of the home, and the
nature of major social institutions like church and school. We
have also probably slighted developments and practices
within the profession of child therapy dear to a particular
reader's heart. No mention has been made, for example, of
the group or family therapies, though they are discussed
elsewhere in this book. The names of many significant figures
within the broad field of child therapy and child welfare
have, perforce, been omitted from this account as well. They
do appear, however, in many of the books and articles on
which this history has been based.

This abbreviated history of child treatment methods re-
minds us that many contemporary therapeutic strategies have
roots far in our past, the products of a particular time, with
its values, beliefs, knowledge, and assumptions. In practice,
however, all child therapies rely on both a healer confident
of his powers, and a child who believes in the healer. It is in
this relationship that the past and present are fused.

References

1. deMause, L. The evolution of childhood. In L. deMause (Ed.),
   History of Childhood. New York: Psychohistory Press, 1974, pp.
   1-73.
2. Zilboorg, G., and Henry, G. W. *A History of Medical Psychology*.
   New York: Norton, 1941.

3. Aries, P. *Centuries of Childhood*. New York: Knopf, 1962.
4. Neugebauer, R. Medieval and early modern theories of mental illness. *Archives of General Psychiatry*, 1979, *36*, 477-483.
5. Ruhräh, J. *Pediatrics of the Past*. New York: Hoeber, 1925.
6. Rousseau, J. *The Emile of Jean-Jacques Rousseau: Selections*. (W. Boyd, Trans.) New York: Teachers College Press, 1962.
7. Comenius, J. A. *School of Infancy*. (E. M. Eller [Ed.]) Chapel Hill: University of North Carolina Press, 1956.
8. Locke, J. Some thoughts concerning education. In C. W. Elliott (Ed.), *English Philosophers of the Seventeenth and Eighteenth Centuries*. Harvard Classics, Vol. 37. New York: Collier, 1910, pp. 9-188.
9. Rousseau, J. *Emile, or On Education*. (B. Foxley, Trans.) London: Dent and Sons, 1911.
10. Seguin, E. *Idiocy: And Its Treatment By the Physiological Method*. New York: William Wood and Co., 1866.
11. Jimack, P. D. Introduction. In C. Brooks, *The Practice of Autosuggestion By the Method of Emile Cové*. (Rev. Ed.) New York: Dodd, Mead, 1922, pp. v-xxviii.
12. Itard, J. *The Wild Boy of Aveyron*. (G. Humphrey and M. Humphrey, Trans.) New York: Appleton-Century, 1932.
13. Seguin, E. *Traitement Moral, Hygiène et Éducation des Idiots et des Autres Enfants Arrières*. Paris: J. B. Baillière, 1846.
14. See citation 10.
15. Crommelinck, C. *Rapport sur les Hospices d'Aliénés de l'Angleterre, de la France, et de l'Allemagne*. Paris: Courtrai, 1842.
16. Darwin, C. A biographical sketch of an infant. *Mind*, 1877, *2*, 285-294.
17. See citation 15.
18. Ellenberger, H. F. *The Discovery of the Unconscious*. New York: Basic Books, 1970.
19. Coué, E. *Self Mastery Through Conscious Autosuggestion*. (A. S. Van Orden, Trans.) New York: Malkan, 1922.
20. Brooks, C. *The Practice of Autosuggestion By the Method of Emile Coué*. (Rev. Ed.) New York: Dodd, Mead, 1922.
21. Dubois, P. *The Psychic Treatment of Nervous Disorders (The Psychoneuroses and Their Moral Treatment)*. (S. E. Jelliffe and W. A. White, Trans. and Ed.) New York: Funk & Wagnalls, 1905.

22. Key, E. *The Century of the Child*. (M. Franzos, Trans.) New York: Putnam, 1909.

23. Kern, S. Freud and the birth of child psychiatry. *Journal of the History of the Behavioral Sciences*, 1973, *9*(4), 360-368.

24. Freud, S. Analysis of a phobia in a five-year-old boy. In J. Strachey (Ed.), *The Standard Edition of the Complete Psychological Works of Sigmund Freud*. Vol. 10. London: Hogarth Press, 1955, pp. 3-149.

25. von Hug-Hellmuth, H. Zur Technik der Kinderanalyse [On the technique of child analysis]. *International Journal of Psycho-Analysis*, 1921, *2*, 287-305.

26. Klein, M. *The Psychoanalysis of Children*. London: Hogarth Press, 1932.

27. Freud, A. *Introduction to the Technique of Child Analysis*. Washington, D.C.: Nervous and Mental Disease Publishing Co., 1928.

28. Levy, D. *Studies in Sibling Rivalry: Research Monographs No. 2*. New York: American Orthopsychiatric Association, 1937.

29. Conn, J. H. The play interview: A method of studying children's attitudes. *American Journal of the Diseases of Children*, 1939, *58*, 1199-1214.

30. Solomon, J. C. Active play therapy. *American Journal of Orthopsychiatry*, 1938, *8*, 479-498.

31. Levy, D. Trends in therapy: III. Release therapy. *American Journal of Orthopsychiatry*, 1939, *9*, 713-736.

32. Taft, J. *The Dynamics of Therapy in a Controlled Relationship*. New York: Macmillan, 1933.

33. Allen, F. *Psychotherapy with Children*. New York: Norton, 1942.

34. Axline, V. M. *Play Therapy*. Chicago: Houghton-Mifflin, 1947.

35. Dorfman, E. Play therapy. In C. R. Rogers (Ed.), *Client-Centered Therapy*. Boston: Houghton Mifflin, 1951, pp. 235-277.

36. Levine, M., and Wishner, J. The case records of the psychological clinic at the University of Pennsylvania (1896-1961). *Journal of the History of the Behavioral Sciences*, 1977, *13*, 59-66.

37. O'Donnell, J. M. The clinical psychology of Lightner Witmer: A Case Study of Institutional Innovation and Intellectual Change. *Journal of the History of Behavioral Sciences*, 1979, *15*, 3-17.

38. Gianascol, A. J. Historical introduction [Lightner Witmer's

"What I did with Don"]. In S. A. Szurek and I. N. Berlin, (Eds.), *Clinical Studies in Childhood Psychoses*. New York: Brunner/Mazel, 1973, pp. 48-50.

39. Witmer, L. Practical work in psychology. *Pediatrics,* 1896, *2,* 462-471.
40. Healy, W. *The Individual Delinquent.* Boston: Little, Brown, 1915.
41. Hetznecker, W., and Forman, M. A. Community child psychiatry: Evolution and direction. *American Journal of Orthopsychiatry,* 1971, *41* (3), 350-360.
42. Noshpitz, J. The history of residential treatment. Unpublished manuscript, Children's Hospital, Washington, D.C., 1972.
43. Maudsley, H. *The Physiology and Pathology of the Mind.* London: Macmillan, 1867.
44. Emminghaus, H. *Die Psychischen Storeungen des Kindesalters.* Tübingen: Laupp, 1887.
45. Bender, L. Emerging patterns in child psychiatry. *Bulletin of the New York Academy of Medicine,* 1958, *34*(12) 794-810.
46. Potter, H. W. Schizophrenia in children. *American Journal of Psychiatry,* 1933, *12,* 1253-1270.
47. Watson, J. B. *Psychology from the Point of View of a Behaviorist.* Philadelphia: Lippincott, 1919.
48. Senn, M. J. E. Insights on the child development movement in the United States. *Monographs of the Society for Research in Child Development,* 1975, *40,* 3-4. [Whole Serial No. 161]
49. Watson, J. B., and Watson, R. R. Studies in infant psychology. *Scientific Monthly,* 1921, *13,* 493-515.
50. Jones, M. C. A Laboratory study of fear: The case of Peter. *Pedagogical Seminary,* 1924, *31,* 308-315.
51. Mowrer, O. H., and Mowrer, W. M. Enuresis—A method for its study and treatment. *American Journal of Orthopsychiatry,* 1938, *8,* 436-459.
52. Weiner, J. M., and Jaffe, S. A historical overview of childhood psychopharmacology. In J. M. Weiner (Ed.), *Psychopharmacology in Childhood and Adolescence*. New York: Basic Books, 1977, pp. 9-40.
53. Bradley, C. The behavior of children receiving benzedrine. *American Journal of Psychiatry,* 1937, *94,* 577-585.

54. Cutts, K. K., and Jasper, H. H. Effect of benzedrine sulfate and phenobarbital on behavior problem children with abnormal electroencephalograms. *Archives of Neurology and Psychiatry*, 1939, *41*, 1138-1145.

55. Molitch, M., and Eccles, A. K. The effect of benzedrine sulfate on the intelligence scores of children. *American Journal of Psychiatry*, 1937, *94*, 587-590.

56. Molitch, M., and Sullivan, J. P. The effect of benzedrine sulfate on children taking the new Standard Achievement Test. *American Journal of Orthopsychiatry*, 1937, *7*, 519-522.

57. Molitch, M., and Poliakoff, S. The effect of benzedrine sulfate on enuresis. *Archives of Pediatrics*, 1937, *54*, 499-501.

58. Bender, L., and Cottington, F. The use of amphetamine sulfate (benzedrine) in child psychiatry. *American Journal of Psychiatry*, 1942, *99*, 116-121.

3

BASIC INGREDIENTS OF THE THERAPEUTIC SITUATION

> Our survey has suggested that much, if not all, of the effectiveness of different forms of psychotherapy may be due to those features that all have in common rather than to those that distinguish them from each other. . . . Since the leading theories of psychotherapy represent alternative rather than incompatible formulations, it is unlikely that any one of them is completely wrong. The activity stimulated by the class of psychotherapeutic doctrines will eventually yield sufficient information either to prove that they are all, to all practical purposes, identical or to clarify and substantiate differences between them.
>
> Jerome Frank[1]

The many forms of psychotherapy for children range from the witch doctor, with his rituals for lifting a curse, to the behavior therapist establishing his hierarchies; from the short-term, directed, and goal-oriented therapist strengthening existing defenses and achieving symptom relief, to the analyst employing play techniques that challenge the child's defenses and his assumptions regarding himself and others. The family therapist, using a very different approach, does not focus on the child at all but rather sees the child as a thermometer of family group tensions—the problems he must attack.

All forms of therapy for children attempt to influence the youngster to make changes in three areas—cognition, emotion, and overt behavior. These are the essential ingredients

47

common to all. Some emphasize one much more than the others: The dynamic insight therapist, concerned primarily with cognitive and emotional spheres, expects that behavior will change as a consequence of changes in these; the behavior therapist believes that influencing behavior is primary, that attitudes and feelings will change as a result of a behavioral emphasis.

The three ingredients—behavior, thought, emotion—are influenced in a series of delineated stages or phases, phases that overlap and vary enormously in emphasis and time spent in them, depending on the particular technique being considered. We may conceptualize the stages as follows:

• Establishing the working relationship
• Analysis of the problem and its cause
• An explanation of the problem
• Establishing and implementing the formula for change
• Termination

ESTABLISHING THE WORKING RELATIONSHIP

Hope, the expectation of help and belief in a helping person, is a key to this phase. Independent of the type of therapy, this ingredient itself is responsible for rapidly relieving symptoms. Significant improvement in social functioning, however, is a separate phenomenon. It varies considerably depending upon the therapeutic goals and results, and is much more dependent upon the length of contact between patient and therapist.

In this stage of setting up a working relationship, we see the development of the therapist's understanding and responding to the child (and family) and to the child's needs, both overt and latent. With children, this stage may be more prolonged than with adults because specific gratification may be needed for the youngster to develop the required incentive. The child, in contrast to the adult patient, usually does not come to treatment of his own accord. A child may need time to form the attitude that the therapist is a person who is important to him and who can be helpful in other ways, a person who knows more about the "problem" than he or his parents do, or at least knows more about what the problem is and can come up with a solution. The degree and intensity of "authoritativeness" either invested in or assumed by different therapists ranges widely from the therapist who remains at a distance and assumes magical or supernatural powers to the therapist who regresses to the youngster's level of thinking and feeling.

Different societies and cultures not only determine how symptoms are defined but also, in many cases, the treatments for them and the nature of the therapist-patient relationship. At one extreme, a society that sanctions possession by devils as the principal etiological basis for emotional problems will promote exorcism as the effective treatment and hold the therapist in a magical role. At the other end, a society in which personal achievement and independence are valued characteristics tends to promote mutual investigation into the way the individual relates to others. Since the young child in all societies tends to see the external world as magically controlling him or her, a child may have many unrealistic feelings and beliefs about the therapist and the therapist's power. Child therapists from culture to culture find that suggestion "happens" more with child patients than with adult patients. Therapists also seem to find that this first stage of relationship development and the emotional investment attached to it are probably more important for work with children because the "corrective emotional experience" plays such a large role in work with youngsters. "Relationship therapy" began as a mode of helping children.[2] This will be illustrated in the case of Matt and his therapist. The rest of this section will be devoted to the progression of "relationship therapy" through this particular example.

Matt was a nine-year-old fourth grader who was seen because his school work was rapidly deteriorating during the year following his parents' divorce. He daydreamed in school, drew pictures in class, and told tall stories; his fantasy life appeared to replace a painful real world.

First session

Therapist: "Okay, Matt, now you've told me about all the things you like to do and all about that soccer game you were in last week. How about things you don't like to do? This is the place we can talk about anything and everything, including stuff that's *not* so much fun. I guess your mom has already told you that that's my business, I'm a 'worry doctor'."

Matt: "Well . . . I don't like math. The teacher always picks on me. She's an old fart! Wait a minute! Who told you I was having trouble in school anyway?"

Therapist: "Well, I've talked to your teacher to get an idea of how things are going from her point of view, but *you're* the one I really want to talk with. Maybe when you get to know me a little better we can talk about it more. I think you're probably worried about it and worried about yourself, too. Anyhow, now, let's draw some pictures. I hear you like to spend time in school drawing pictures."

Matt: (Excitedly) "Yeah!"

Matt proceeds to draw a detailed picture of two monsters fighting and eating up the world. He keeps glancing at the therapist as if expecting disapproval, but instead gets only interest.

Therapist: "This is a good place to draw those pictures. Let's make up stories about them, too."

Matt: "Okay."

Therapist: "How come it's easy to do this and so hard to do math?"

Matt: "Sometimes my brain gets heavy. Like it's stuck in the mud?"

Therapist: "What would you do if you were really stuck in the mud?"

Matt: "I'd just sit in the car and go to sleep. No, maybe I'd call the gas station first to come and help—sometimes those guys can pull you out."

ANALYSIS OF THE PROBLEM AND ITS CAUSE

In the second stage, problem analysis, the symptoms or behaviors to be influenced are selected. The work shifts to a more cognitive level of goal selection. Problem analysis always relates to the life experience of the patient and involves some self-revelation regarding present functioning and past behavior. The examination of the youngster's life experience can be broad and unstructured, or narrowly focused according to the conceptual framework of the therapist. It is often a search for "the cause." The causes may be found by recreating the problems, reinterpreting events of the past, or sometimes even inventing causes. Many feel that the effectiveness of the treatment to follow is ultimately related to the degree to which the child patient participates in the process of inquiry. Hence, it is probable that the durability of success may co-vary with the youngster's actively choosing the conceptual framework or viewpoint of the therapist rather than passively submitting to it.

Several sessions later

Therapist: ". . . Well Matt, how's math going?"

Matt: "Terrible!"

Therapist: "Why?"

Matt: "I think there's a nerve that's cracked in my brain where the numbers are, the nerve that goes down to my mouth."

Therapist: "Oh, how come?"

Matt: "Probably it happened when I had to have those stitches taken in my chin when I was staying with my grandparents last year. It took three guys to hold me down! You know something else? I think that broken nerve makes my brain feel heavy, too. And it goes to my hand. I get this funny feeling in my hand. It wants to scribble all over the math paper."

Therapist: "When you fell down and got the stitches, weren't you at your grandparents because your mom and dad were getting divorced?"

Matt: "Yeah."

Therapist: "And that's when something went wrong with your brain."

Matt: "That's what it seems like."

Therapist: "Maybe that's when things that were going wrong began to get mixed up in math too, like when your hand wants to do something on its own, and gets out of control. That must have been a very tough time."

Matt: "Yeah, nobody seemed to know what was happening or what to do."

AN EXPLANATION OF THE PROBLEM

The explanation or interpretation of the problem may occur, as do the other phases, over a variable time span and be emphasized in one form of therapy over others. In many cases, the explanation must also be extended to the child's family in order to prepare the way for altered behavior toward him. In nonliterate belief systems, a simple explanation is proffered—that the patient is the victim of a curse or a devil because of some act that offended ancestors or spirits. Explanation is brief in behavior therapy, lengthy in psychoanalysis. Explanation in the latter may be indirect through the use of play materials or stories but verbal interchange always enhances explanation.

In order for the child patient to be willing to learn about himself and to undergo change, he must be convinced that the therapist's formulation is one which he can adopt. For that reason, this phase is often considered to be an educative or learning experience and has strong affective or emotional substance to hold it together. If the ideas between therapist and child differ, they are sometimes reconciled by the patient "coming around" and accepting the therapist's notions. However, as in the previous phase, it is generally felt that therapy is most effective if the therapist's ideas are not imposed, but new ones are mutually sought and developed with some initiative afforded by the child patient.

During this period there continues to be an attempt to split off the symptoms so that the youngster can look at them as separate from himself. This reinforces the therapeutic alliance, because the child patient may merge with or identify with the "power and knowledge" of the therapist for a period of time in order to gain control over the symptoms or to encapsulate them. Contained within this phase is the so-called "corrective emotional experience," which may be a more crucial phenomenon with youngsters than with adults. Probably a common ingredient in all forms of therapy with children is the sense of newness—a novel experience—with a new person incorporated into the youngster's life, along with a reordering of behaviors and coping patterns based on that fresh new look.

The phenomenon of "insight" is considered by some to be crucial to this phase. Insight ranges all the way from understanding complicated unconscious reasons for illness (uncommon in children), to "learning" that one has assumed maladaptive ways of behaving, or to understanding the nature of a curse or possession. Insight is really an acceptance and incorporation of the explanation of the cause of the problem. It can be experienced as self-understanding, and can be arrived at by the child either directly or symbolically, or through utilizing the therapist's "insight" which the patient accepts as his own. It may involve a confrontation with himself as others see him, as well as with himself as "another person," for example, as someone who stopped growing at an earlier age because of unconscious carry-over to the present.

Several sessions later

Therapist: "Boy, the monsters in those pictures just keep doing the same things, Matt, tearing each other apart and eating up the world."

Matt: (Laughs) "Yeah, all those little people in the world are getting zapped."

Therapist: "I'll bet sometimes part of you feels like that."

Matt: "Like what?"

Therapist: "Like being little and bashed around by big people."

Matt: "No. I pretend to be the monsters."

Therapist: "Well, I guess if you can't beat 'em, join 'em. Is that why you get in fights at school with kids so much this year?"

Matt: "Yeah."

Therapist: "So you don't just draw pictures of monsters, you play them out too."

Matt: "Yeah, it used to be more fun just to draw."

Therapist: "I guess you're beginning to realize how mad you really are, from drawing those monsters fighting each other."

Matt: "You know, sometimes my hand wants to scribble all over those monsters when I'm doing them?"

Therapist: "Just like math?"

Matt: "Yeah, it feels like it wants to break loose. It's kind of scary."

Therapist: "Maybe your arm is mad. Maybe it's mad about those monsters fighting each other. But how come it overflowed to math. Was math your good subject?"

Matt: "No, it's my dad's. But I don't see him anymore."

Therapist: "I guess it's easier for your arm to be mad at big people like your dad than for you to be, huh? Is it about the divorce and his going away?"

Matt: (Angrily) "Well, if they were going to get divorced, why did they ever have me? And why doesn't he care? Why did he go away and move to another place and leave me with my mom? She's always picking on me."

Therapist: "Like your math teacher?"

ESTABLISHING AND IMPLEMENTING THE FORMULA FOR CHANGE

The last ingredient is to follow the "prescription," which includes what must be done in order to get better. It may be a prescription for the child, the family, and others. It may include the number of times that something in particular must be done in order to effect improvement. The patient will be told that the improvement will depend upon his doing or saying certain things, holding certain thoughts or feelings. It is during this period that behavioral components begin to replace the cognitive and emotional ones which received emphasis earlier in therapy; knowledge, now, is put into practice. However, the formula and instructions usually evoke a strong emotional response which must be managed if it is to produce behavior that is more adaptive and more durable than previous patterns. Therapies, such as behavior therapy, presuming that cognitive and emotional factors will change *after* behavior is influenced in a directive fashion, quickly strive to reach this phase. Others rely heavily on the development of cognitive and emotional change and assume that behavioral change will follow. This period includes different degrees of activity and responsibility by the therapist and the patient alike, such as working to achieve change, and translating insight into action.

It is this stage which brings about changes in the child's life. The process of change itself becomes more open and fluid than the child's therapist may have foreseen. Shifts occur in the perspectives of both child and therapist. A therapist who was previously committed to a behavior therapy viewpoint might find the healing process itself becoming more "dynamic." Children may want "help with problems" rather than being rewarded with tokens for right behavior. Or, a psychotherapist may actively gratify a child in the manner of a behavior therapist, all in the interest of serving the child. During this very active portion of the treatment process, numerous readjustments and accommodations transpire. The therapist shifts in understanding, in theory and meta-theory, in formulation, revisions, and consensuses, and in praxis, because the therapist is responsive to his sharing in the vital process along with the child. The prescription is filled realistically, modified to be in harmony with new insights and a new set of relationships. Likewise, the child changes more and more and finds the therapist's vantage point more attractive. Actual experiencing seems to overshadow the therapist's "school" or theoretical conceptualizations, as well as the child's style of living that had crystallized earlier in the child's life before therapy started.

Sometimes this therapeutic work can be done directly and exclusively with the individual child. Usually, however, there is a need for explanation and instructions to the family and other persons in the child's milieu, for example, school personnel. Here the therapist participates and mediates as a helper between the patient and the milieu, the ecosphere the child lives in. Sometimes the therapist makes it clear that the process of change is largely in the hands of those who surround the child and that they must carry the main burden of the treatment.

Several sessions later

Therapist: "There are lots of things you've wanted to say about the divorce, about your mom and dad, but how are things going at school?"

Matt: "Okay. My arm is better. And the teacher has stopped picking on me."

Therapist: "I guess you've got more energy to put into math now that we're really talking about that part of you, your arm, that was so mad."

Matt: "No. It's not that. I'm just sick of drawing monster pictures. Look I drew a picture of a family getting a divorce."

Therapist: "The father is way off at the edge. Do you mean he ought to be more involved?"

Matt: "Yeah, I wish my father would see me sometimes."

The therapist got in touch with the father who came back for a visit. During his discussion with the father, the father's overcontrol and anger at his own father, and his inability to know how to be a father, began to emerge. He agreed to come back regularly to visit with Matt and have Matt visit him in the summers. He talked over how to be a father and things to do with his son.

TERMINATION

This last phase is the test of whether the actual therapeutic work has succeeded, has "taken" so to speak, and has so improved adjustment that healthy changes can continue independent of the therapist's direct presence. The work toward independence from the therapist begins at the start of some forms of therapy, particularly when a termination date is set. For example, in brief therapy a series of procedures or steps is outlined as constituting the treatment, and a goal such as specific treatment relief is set from the start as the endpoint. In many forms of therapy, termination depends greatly on the child and his family's acceptance of a mutually satisfactory balance of mastery over certain problems with adjustment to, or acceptance of, others.

Several sessions later

The father had become much more free and he and Matt began to have fun together for the first time. The stiffness in their relationship had disappeared. They did lots of hiking and horsing around together on visits. The father indicated he had gotten to know Matt for the first time. He said to the therapist: "Funny isn't it, after I got divorced I finally learned how to be a father. But I guess I really never learned when I was a kid what a father was like."

Therapist: "Well, Matt, what shall we do today?"

Matt: "Is there some place we could go outside and throw a ball. I'd like to show you what a good pitcher I am. My arm is really working."

Therapist: "Sure."

Matt: "By the way, I don't want to hurt your feelings, but how many more times do I have to come here?"

Therapist: "How many more do you want to come?"

Matt: "Well . . . I guess maybe three or four anyway."

Therapist: "Let's make it four more times. I think you're ready to go it on your own. But you might get some feelings about stopping our appointments, or even feel like it's *me* leaving you. So we have some time to talk about them just in case they should happen to occur now that we've set a date for saying good-bye. And, of course, you can always come back later for a checkup."

A GENERAL CONSIDERATION— THE PERSONALITY OF THE THERAPIST

Throughout discussion of the generic stages of therapy we posited the hidden qualities of the therapist's personality, for after all personality is the vehicle, the instrument, through which the method is shaped. The common denominators for effective therapists will most likely include; (a) a concern for the child patient; (b) an ability to get inside the youngster's head in imagination and to think and feel developmentally with him at his own level in order to communicate effectively; and (c) an expectation of success related to the influence of the therapist's own personality.

References

1. Frank, J. *Persuasion and Healing: A Comparative Study of Psychotherapy.* (Rev. Ed.) Baltimore, MD: Johns Hopkins University, 1961.
2. Allen, F. H. *Psychotherapy with Children.* New York: Norton, 1942.

4

WHO HEALS DISTURBED CHILDREN?

Putting the therapist-patient relationship in an historical as well as humanistic perspective, Bugental has written:

> The psychotherapist's ancestors are the medicine man, the wizard, the priest, the family doctor. In every age, man has needed to have someone to turn to to help him in contending with the awful unknownness of his fate. Inevitable, invariably, the one turned to has been invested by others and by himself with supranormal vision and potency. This has usually been both his greatest reward and his most terrifying burden. Certainly this is so for the psychotherapist today.[1]

Aside from the neurotic excesses to which some psychotherapists are prey, Bugental has named certain "synergic gratifications" that accrue for the therapist: seizing the occasion to live fully as a participant observer in the human condition, growing personally as a result of the therapeutic relationship, indulging a profound fascination for psychological processes in their natural habitat, and feeling some pride in one's successful attempts to help patients "emerge." Certainly, these apply to the child therapist.

Bugental described a series of characteristics of the more mature and, presumably, more gifted psychotherapist. Humility is required because one's knowledge, skills, and grasp are always partial. The therapist, far from being aloof, should be a model of "presence" and authenticity for his patient. "Selective participation" refers to the ability to say just enough and no more, together with the right timing. The phrase, "changing conceptuum," implies that the therapist recognizes the need to change and learn continually. In varying degrees, therapists cannot avoid obtaining some neurotic gratification from doing treatment, and must be able to accept the realistic guilt associated with this realization, as well as the neurotic guilt attending even unavoidable failure.

There have been four general approaches to describing the personality of the healer who carries out psychotherapeutic work with children. The first dwells on the healing personality in terms that one can only call "overly idealistic." The second is the pragmatic and behavioral orientation. The third focuses on the perceptual and cognitive style of the healer, while the fourth emphasizes certain personality traits that, in theory if not fully in practice, are susceptible to operational definition.

THE OVERLY IDEALISTIC PRESCRIPTION

The healing personality is all too often described in moralistic and sentimental terms. One child therapist, for example, stated that the ultimate purpose of treatment is to put both child and therapist into a closer relationship with God. "Above all," he wrote, "[the healer must have] a loving spirit, a willingness to give, and the relinquishing of considerations of self."[2] Another list of traits included intelligence, honesty, reliability, and sufficient professional and cultural training.[3] The early formulations of Strupp[4] showed similar idealistic inexactness. He advanced the following personal features as the mark of a therapeutic person: personal integrity, humanity, dedication, and patience. Canon,[5] in contrast, believed that autonomy, alienation, withdrawal, and guardedness were the important features of a therapeutic personality.

None of these prescriptions brings us nearer to an understanding of the personality best fitted for the work of healing young children. The specifications listed by Sachs[6] would seem to be more relevant to the enterprise of at least psychodynamic child psychotherapy. Sachs included: (a) access to and wish to know his own unconscious; (b) some neurotic problems; (c) some personality integration and strength; and (d) skepticism about any shortcuts to treatment.

THE BEHAVIORAL DEFINITION

A second approach to the healing personality has been to define the healer's gifts operationally, pinning down the behavioral qualities of the "effective" or "competent" therapist and bypassing debates about the inner heart of the healer.

Strupp,[7] for example, studied what therapists actually did during sessions. His numerous findings were provocative. Therapists who had been analyzed for more than 500 hours, he discovered, were not very different in behavior from those who had 250 hours of analysis or even less. Freudians and neo-Freudians were indistinguishable in their actions. When compared to residents in psychiatry, psychoanalysts made more interpretative and fewer exploratory comments but took more initiative with patients than did the residents. Older and more experienced therapists of all schools propounded gloomier prognoses than did inexperienced ones.

Strupp's data suggested to him that therapists, based on their behavior and inferred attitudes in the experimental situation, are of two kinds:

> Group I therapists appear to be more tolerant, more humane, more permissive, more "democratic," and more "therapeutic." Group II therapists emerge as more directive, disciplinarian, moralistic and harsh (p. 65).

Most empirical studies of therapist behavior have relied upon ratings by judges of diverse backgrounds and competencies; each rates the behavior of a therapist according to his own reference system. Only with difficulty can one who is a practitioner conceive of an ideal therapist without including his own idealized self-picture, an amalgamation of fantasy and reality. If a rater values safety or passivity by the therapist more than activity, he will consider the more energetic or zealous therapist as less competent than one who keeps quiet and at least tries to "do no harm."

PERCEPTUAL AND COGNITIVE STYLE

A third approach to identifying the healing person is exemplified by the work of Combs and Soper,[8] who studied the perceptual organization of 29 counselors:

> Effective relationships seem dependent upon the nature of the helper's attitudes and ways of perceiving himself, his task, his client and his purposes. . . . Apparently, what makes an effective professional worker is a question not of what methods he uses, but of how well he has learned to use his unique self as an instrument for working with other people (p. 222).

Soper calls this the "self as instrument" concept of the professional worker.

> If the professional worker is one who has learned to use his unique self effectively, then the failure to find any common behavioral characteristics among such persons is precisely what we would predict. The search for common uniqueness is obviously foredoomed to failure (p. 222).

Combs and Soper found much higher correlations between the perceptual patterns of the counselors and their effectiveness (as rated by independent judges) than had been reported previously between similar ratings and any behavioral measures.

In their humanistic stance, Combs and Soper were not alone during the 1960s. Among Freudian psychoanalysts, one of the most crisply outspoken was Sacha Nacht,[9] the Parisian analyst, who held that it was the real person of the analyst (the "self beyond roles," as Otto Rank had termed it) which contributed the greatest curative factor. Nacht insisted that it was not professional role-playing, aloofness, or even benevolent neutrality which helped to heal disturbed people, but the person of the therapist, in the here and now. Proclaiming the necessity for the analyst's attitude to be authentic and not contrived, Nacht advanced the view that "the self is an instrument of healing":

> And it can only be so if the analyst possesses an open-heartedness as nearly perfect as possible, arising above all from his unconscious, enabling him to be spontaneously and intuitively what he should be at any given moment in the actual analytical situation. His attitude should respond to the immediate ongoing process, then, and should not have been premeditated. It is in this regard so necessary that the analyst, himself the sole instrument of his technique, should possess a disposition of openness and flexibility. This will enable him to work within the indispensable framework of technical principles and yet create from the analyst/analysand dialogue a living relationship between one particular person and another (p. 208).

Jules V. Coleman[10] had said much the same thing some fifteen years before:

> Actually, the doctor-patient relationship is not a tool or instrument of psychotherapy; it is the primary process itself. It is the stage and the play, and not merely the way the lines are read. Unfortunately, the psychiatrist in train-

ing too often conceives of psychotherapy as a specific technique or group of techniques rather than, in its most fundamental aspect, as an experience in human relationship and understanding.

The following case illustrates this point. A fourteen-year-old white girl from a Roman Catholic household was speaking, in the penultimate session of her psychotherapy, about what she would remember of the therapy ten years afterward:

"I came to you when I was twelve and I had already been starving myself for a year. I'll always remember how I was at that time because I think you helped me to be different. *Then* I thought my feelings were just there occasionally, but I had no right to have them or to be interested in them. I was doing what I thought I ought to do but you helped me to do different(ly). You were the first grownup I ever met who cared how things really were inside me, my dreams, my private thoughts and feelings. I never knew, then, that I could look inside if I want to and have my own feelings and beliefs. I didn't feel I had the right and I didn't feel it made any difference how I felt. I'll never skip over my dreams again. I like to see what they mean. I thought I just had to act a part and do what other people expected from me. You were on my side, I knew, but it was a side I didn't even know I had. I'll remember that for ten years, and probably forever."

SOME PERSONALITY CHARACTERISTICS

The fourth approach would emphasize the personality of the therapist, although rarely in North American child psychiatry does one find a statement about the "aura" of the healer. Still, reason and plausibility remind us that some child therapists *are* more gifted than others.

Since the therapist uses his "self" as the major implement of help, it is important to know what the therapeutic "self" is and how it can be characterized. Although much of what follows is based on the wisdom of clinical experience, there is good reason to believe that the personal qualities to be discussed are measurable.

The ability to inspire confidence

Some therapists inspire confidence in a broad spectrum of suffering children, while others can "make it" with only a few. Many therapists choose to work with selected cases. They often find themselves shunning the severely ill or antisocial child, for example, while prizing the neurotic. Some, recognizing that they are most effective in treating inhibited or neurotic children, may pass on to colleagues those children who are aggressive, action-oriented, and relatively nonverbal. Those who "act out" are often eliminated from a practice in favor of those who "act in."

Child therapists often console (and congratulate) themselves with the truism that nobody can do all things equally well and that it is enough to recognize one's therapeutic limitations.

Therapeutic zeal

Sachs[11] followed Freud in derogating therapeutic zeal and valuing a degree of skepticism among candidates for analytic training:

> Freud warned repeatedly against what he called *furor sanandi*—therapeutic overeagerness. To those who are impatient for quick therapeutic effects, psychoanalytic technique will soon become a burden because it is neither apt to gratify nor to assuage their compassion. To them the great body of psychoanalytic theory, so much greater than in any other psychotherapeutic method, will appear to be so much deadweight. The long duration of the psychoanalytic process

with the great amount of patience, which it demands from
patient and therapist alike, will be unendurable for
them. . . . In an extreme form this type is represented by
"miracle workers," hypernarcissistic cranks for whom psychotherapy is an enticing field of operation. These are easily recognizable and ought to be weeded out at once (p.
162).

Zeal, however, seems to be the crucial quality for convert-
ing a businesslike, rather humdrum therapist into a charismatic healer. Zeal is probably more directly communicated
to children than to other patients. For the child, the uplift
of morale comes in being understood.

Some child psychoanalysts report that when they were
young practitioners they experienced countertransferences
which were more parental and therefore more generative of
hope for the growing child. Then, as they grew older, they
began to perceive themselves in the role of a grandparent.[12]
As zeal diminishes, perhaps, hope fades and the orientation
to help shifts from children to older age groups. Child psychiatrists sometimes have reported that they felt they were—at
the onset of their careers—more supple both physically and
mentally than "adult psychiatrists." As they grew older, however, they found themselves shifting to a practice that focused
less on the child and more on the parents.

Although it might be said that child therapists "grow up,"
experiencing a waning of hope and zeal as they get older,
there are notable exceptions. One need only think of Anna
Freud, Lucy Jessner, David Levy, William Langford, Frances
Wickes, Frederick Allen, and Virginia Axline, for example,
to show that it is not always the case that therapists, as they
grow older, are drawn to an older age group for their ex-
clusive clientele.

Perhaps middle-aged child therapists do *not* in fact abandon the field to their juniors. In a recent survey of 72 grad-

uates of the Philadelphia Child Guidance Clinic taken many years after their training, only one reported that he now saw adults exclusively in his practice.[13]

The ability to tolerate ambiguity

Zeal and commitment, however praiseworthy, must coexist within the healer along with the capability of living with tentativeness and ambiguity. The person with a healing personality is willing to work enthusiastically with hypotheses that are tentative, and with an imperfect and impermanent truth unfolding at the end of the most laborious efforts.

Some therapists evade ambiguity by subscribing to rigid techniques and outlawing any maneuvers that do not fit into their therapeutic orthodoxy. Others, equally uncomfortable with anything less than certainty, try to scrap theory entirely. They retreat eagerly into counting behaviors and quantifying elements of psychotherapy. An evolving and flexible theory—always growing, remaining open and modifiable, and ever subject to confirmation, disconfirmation, and recasting—is difficult for some therapists of children to accomplish. They prefer the support of orthodoxy, faith, and certitude.

Flexibility

Flexibility can be attitudinal as well as musculoskeletal. Some therapists are truly eclectic and can go further than others of their colleagues in identifying the problems of a given child and setting up and carrying out the variety of treatment plans required for different children.

This kind of flexibility is not universally accepted or aspired to among child therapists. Some feel that intentionally multifaceted work is tantamount to therapeutic nihilism. However, when observing what therapists actually do, there seems to be more flexibility in their actual practice than would seem to be indicated in their particular school of orientation. To deal with parents as well as with children, even more flexibility is needed. Take the following case:

> A male child psychiatrist, 33 years old, saw a six-year-old girl in his private practice. The girl was afraid her mother would kill her. The child psychiatrist speculated that the child was projecting her own rage onto her mother; he thought the very next phase in treatment should consist of demonstrating to the little girl that her mother had no leanings toward infanticide. He reasoned that if the child were not alienated from the family system, she would lose her fear of annihilation, and so initiated a period of family therapy.
>
> In these family group sessions, it became clear that the mother *did* wish to kill her daughter and actively feared that she would do so. The therapist decided to leave aside the family group approach temporarily and concentrate on mother and daughter, to help the mother to be more assertive as a disciplinarian and teacher and to encourage the little girl to have her feelings and discuss them as she and her mother began to try out some new ways of relating to each other.
>
> When the mother was less tentative as a disciplinarian, she ceased to be infanticidal and the little girl's play showed her fantasy world became peopled with good witches.

In this case, the therapist utilized individual, family, and parent-child therapy.

Although described as an essential feature of dynamic and analytic approaches to child treatment, empathy is probably a major element in almost any psychological therapy and a central tool for facilitating the therapeutic alliance. Many authors[14-19] have suggested that we sometimes call upon empathy as an aid to understanding our patients when our intellect in its pure form fails.

What is "empathy"? The literature abounds in definitions, with that of Greenson[20] being the most concise:

> Empathy means to share, to experience the feelings of another human being. One partakes of a quality of feelings and not the quantity. Its motive in psychoanalysis is to give understanding; it is not used for vicarious pleasure.

Greenson has differentiated between sympathy and empathy and held that condolence, agreement, and pity are necessary for sympathy, but not for empathy. According to Olden,[21] empathy "is the capacity of the subject instinctively and intuitively to feel as the object does. It is a process of the ego" (p. 112). Schafer,[22] who theorized about a hierarchy of empathic possibilities, suggested that the highest form is a "generative" one in which

> the subject, so far as his own experience goes, feels that he is one with the object; he feels what the object feels; and yet above all, out of self interest as well as interest in the object, he maintains his individuality and perspective at the same time (p. 153).

Empathy is a quality that has interest for other schools of therapy as well. Rogers[23] described the concept in the following terms:

> To sense the client's private world as if it were your own, but without ever losing the "as if" quality—this is empathy, and this seems essential to therapy. To sense the client's anger, fear, or confusion as if it were your own, yet without your own anger, fear or confusion getting bound up in it, is the condition we are endeavoring to describe. When the client's world is this clear to the therapist, and he moves about in it free, then he can both communicate his understanding of what is clearly known to the client and can also

voice meanings in the client's experience of which the client
is scarcely aware. (p. 99).

A person who has lost the ability to imagine and remember
childhood in all its substages would obviously have problems
in developing empathy with a child patient. Someone who
repudiates the child's entire condition as so powerless, bizarre, or meaningless as to lack human merit would also have
formidable barriers to empathy with a given youngster. Empathy is the area where positive regard, trial identification,[24]
and unconditional acceptance merge with positive countertransferences[25] and the myriad distortions which can facilitate
or retard treatment. The capacity for empathy seems at times
to be almost synonymous with the wider notion of the "therapeutic personality." Some appear to have it, while others do
not.

Warmth

Warmth is often considered to be a necessary ingredient in
the therapeutic personality, but research findings have not
confirmed this hypothesis. Among medical therapists, in particular, warmth does not correlate with expertness and success.[26,27] Genuineness and empathy seem to be characteristics
of some competent healers, but not warmth as defined by
the "Non-Possessive Warmth Scale" developed by Truax.[28]
Even genuineness is, in fact, not always attributed to the most
effective therapists; some expert therapists rate low on genuineness scales.

Research evidence about child therapy, as we have noted,
is quite meager. In the guise of "unconditional positive regard" or "nonpossessive warmth," the quality can at least be
reliably rated from audiotapes or videotapes of child psychotherapy sessions,[29-32] some of which show positive cor-

relations between warmth exhibited by the therapist and the outcome of therapy with the child-patient.

Self-knowledge, self-acceptance

Self-knowledge and self-acceptance are qualities often said to characterize the healer. The child's therapist knows himself. He does not act out, project, or deny his inner longings and impulses but knows them and, having made an honest attempt at changing himself, recognizes that there are some things that cannot be changed much more. The therapist understands his own childhood and, in particular, his patterned ways of relating as a child to parents. In short, the healer has most likely devoted careful and lengthy work to personal therapy or analysis.

Self-knowledge, of course, is not always accompanied by increased self-acceptance. If the former can be said to be the nobler virtue, it is nonetheless clear that self-acceptance—which can follow self-knowledge but not precede it—is also important for the therapist. The person who knows himself will accept his own assets and limitations with a certain good humor. He can, when appropriate, be childlike about what he learns and sees, can recognize his own ambivalence, laugh at himself, and laugh with children. He can be accepting and empathetic toward children because he feels that way toward himself. The goal of self-acceptance is not smugness but the ability to make therapeutic use of the self and this use of the self advances far beyond mere self-knowledge.

Awareness of one's limited perspective

As our society becomes more and more heterogeneous and urbanized, the healer's recognition that his outlook is only one of many alternatives assumes increasing relevance for effectiveness in treatment. Knowing the limitations of one's

own outlook is perhaps another aspect of self-understanding.
Take the following example:

> A supervisor reflected as follows on one of the people
> she supervises. This young male therapist, 28 years old, of
> Jewish lower-middle class background, assumes
>
> • all mothers do not work but do relish domesticity
> • all mothers are demonstrative of emotions, are provoc-
>   ative and unsettling, and want to keep a storm agitated
>   in the household
> • all mothers aid their children to become motivated—fueled
>   and driven—by guilty fear
>
> He was always "unmasking" children who were taciturn
> and shy, mothers who were phlegmatic. He thought they
> were being overly defended, neurotically inhibited, avoid-
> ant of competition, and, in short, anything except what
> they appeared to be.
> The supervisor decided that the resident should take on
> work with black children from other ethnic backgrounds
> than his own. The supervisor accompanied the resident on
> school visits and home visits, serving as a kind of "culture
> broker." The resident read ethnographic studies of Ba-
> linese, Alorese, Samoan, Comanche, and Appalachian chil-
> dren. Because of his basic facility for empathy and
> introspection, the resident changed from his previously
> ethnocentric attitudes to attitudes that respected diversity.
> He learned to be more healing.

In former times, it was possible to speak in a facile way of
the dichotomies of right-wrong and sick-well, along with ethical imperatives. When society was simpler and our understanding of a bureaucratized, highly structured society was
much less advanced, we could encourage patients to take on
our values and behavior unquestioningly, for we and they
were of sufficiently similar background for us to anticipate

a final consensus with them. We could urge any adult or child who balked or flinched at assuming his assigned role to "get with it" and to "look within" himself. In simpler days, many therapists tended to accept the institutions of the ruling groups in their societies and to assume that no basic restructuring of the external world was required.

Today, thanks as much to our knowledge of society as to its growing complexity, we can no longer adopt the glibly conservative stance that fitted us in the past. Unless therapists can acknowledge the importance of the outer life as well as the inner, they will lose their credibility, even with quite young children. Differences in age, gender, race, class, and religion are very real and consequential in contemporary society. Harrison and others[33] have demonstrated that the clinician's socioeconomic background influences his view of the child patient—the diagnosis, prognosis, and the recommendations for treatment.

In regard to the therapist's position and viewpoint, special attention should be paid to the status-differential between adult therapist and child patient. The therapist is in a higher, more esteemed position, less "sick" (not a "patient"), older and presumably wiser, and, often, more affluent and socially powerful. Notwithstanding the child therapist's rather democratic style and zeal to know the child, he is "above" the child in status. The differences in age and experience cannot be ignored or denied by the therapist.

The capacity for genuinely adult gratifications

The therapist, it is assumed, is deriving age-specific and age-appropriate pleasure and fulfillment from his daily life. The "synergic" gratifications of sharing in the growth and healing of patient—not unimportant in the whole life economy of the psychotherapists—are by no means simply personal "kicks" from as-if, professional relationships. Healers are childlike, perhaps, but are not children or childish. Engaged in meaningful work from which he does not feel alienated, the therapist also must be involved in give-and-take and sharing-relatedness with beloved persons in his own personal life, such that he has sufficient energy for forming professional relationships with disturbed young children.

The avoidance of anti-parent, anti-sibling bias

Wariness about being anti-parent or anti-sibling seems to be another basic ingredient in the personality of the child healer. No matter how earnest the therapist's determination to empathize with the child, he must not lose sight of the parents. For the child patient, the parents and siblings are real. The therapist must empathize with this fact of life, too. This does not mean, however, that the therapist falls into the trap of "analyzing" the parents or siblings of his patient. Although the child may temporarily desire such partisanship, ultimately the patient wants to have love for his parents. The therapist does not undermine the child's love for the parents, since he knows that such love is an expression of self-esteem.

The child is a growing person and the therapist must have knowledge of normal maturation and emotional development in childhood in order to understand developmental arrest, fixation, regression, and other phenomena. The therapist of a child must be fully cognizant of the growth potential within the child. Admittedly, longitudinal perspective is not always told to the child; a child may feel denigrated, as well as not treated as a unique individual, if the older person, the therapist, talks of the possibilities for outgrowing certain of his present difficulties. The developmental perspective of the adult therapist can be seen by the child as belittling. Preadolescents and adolescents are particularly sensitive to being told they will "outgrow" their "puppy love" or the turbulences that seem so crucial to them. The therapist, imbued with the developmental perspective, derives from it realistic optimism for his work with children. Temporal changes in a salutary environment do bring about helpful changes for many children. If there are not too many strikes against a nine-year-old, he will cope and get to be 10. There are many children, however, who are deeply damaged by internal and outer circumstances; these children do not get better with time only. For them, psychotherapy is necessary, and often also a change in environment.

From our review, it would appear that the healer of disturbed children enters the therapy process more as a humble plodder than a charismatic guru. He is possessed of some traits and attributes that can be studied, taught, and learned. Some mystery remains, but the situation is not totally inexplicable.

References

1. Bugental, J. The person who is the psychotherapist. *Journal of Consulting Psychology*, 1964, *11*, 272-277.
2. Rosenheim, F. Basic attitudes and goals of the therapist. *Mental Hygiene*, 1950, *34*, 400-405.
3. Sachs, H. Observations of a training analyst. *The Psychoanalytic Quarterly*, 1947, *16*, 157-168.
4. Strupp, H. Psychotherapy. *Annual Review of Psychology*, 1962, *13*, 445-448.
5. Canon, H. Personality variables and counselor-client affect. *Journal of Consulting Psychology*, 1964, *11*, 35-41.
6. See citation 3.
7. Strupp, H. The psychotherapist's contribution to the treatment process. *Behavioral Science*, 1958, *3*, 34-67.
8. Combs, A., and Soper, D. The perceptual organization of effective counselors. *Journal of Counseling Psychology*, 1963, *10*, 222-226.
9. Nacht, S. The curative factors in psycho-analysis. *International Journal of Psychoanalysis*, 1962, *43*, 206-211.

10. Coleman, J. V. Patient-physician relationship in psychotherapy. *American Journal of Psychiatry*, 1948, *104*, 638-641.
11. See citation 3.
12. Jessner, L. Training of a child psychiatrist. *Journal of the American Academy of Child Psychiatry*, 1963, *2*, 746-755.
13. Staples, H. Unpublished survey of the Alumni Association of the Philadelphia Child Guidance Clinic while Frederick H. Allen, M.D., was director (1925-1958), 1961-1962.
14. Greenson, R. Empathy and its vicissitudes. *International Journal of Psychoanalysis*, 1960, *41*, 418-424.
15. Loewald, H. Psychoanalytic theory and the psychoanalytic process. *The Psychoanalytic Study of the Child*, 1970, *25*, 45-68.
16. Ornstein, A. Making contact with the inner world of the child: Toward a theory of psychoanalytic psychotherapy with children. *Comparative Psychology*, 1976, *17*, 3-36.
17. Kohut, H. Introspection, empathy, and psychoanalysis: An examination of the relationship between mode of observation and theory. *Journal of the American Psychoanalytic Association*, 1959, *7*, 459-483.
18. Kohut, H. *The Analysis of Self*. New York: International Universities Press, 1971.
19. Fliess, R. The metapsychology of the analyst. *Psychoanalytic Quarterly*, 1942, *11*, 211-227.
20. See citation 14.
21. Olden, C. On adult empathy with children. *The Psychoanalytic Study of the Child*, 1953, *8*, 111-126.
22. Schafer, R. *Aspects of Internalization*. New York: International Universities Press, 1962.
23. Rogers, C. The necessary and sufficient conditions of therapeutic personality change. *Journal of Consulting Psychology*, 1957, *21*, 95-103.
24. See citation 19.
25. Fromm-Reichmann, F. Clinical significance of intuitive processes of the Psychoanalyst. *Journal of the American Psychoanalytic Association*, 1955, *3*, 82-88.
26. See citation 7.
27. Truax, C., and others. Therapist empathy, genuineness, and

warmth and patient therapeutic outcome. *Journal of Consulting Psychology*, 1966, *30*, 395-401.

28. Truax, C. A scale for the measurement of unconditional positive regard. *Psychiatric Institute Bulletin*, 1962, *2* (Issue No. 1).

29. Siegel, C. L. F. Changes in play therapy behavior over time as a function of differing levels of therapist-offered conditions. *Journal of Clinical Psychology*, 1972, *28*, 235-236.

30. Wright, L., Truax, C. B., and Mitchell, K. M. Reliability of process ratings of psychotherapy with children. *Journal of Clinical Psychology*, 1972, *28*, 232-234.

31. Stoffer, D. L. Investigation of positive behavioral change as a function of genuineness, nonpossessive warmth, and empathic understanding. *Journal of Educational Research*, 1970, *63*, 225-228.

32. Truax, C. B., and others. Effects of therapeutic conditions on child therapy. *Journal of Community Psychology*, 1973, *1*, 313-318.

33. Harrison, S. I., and others. Social status and child psychiatric practice: The influence of the clinician's socioeconomic origin. *American Journal of Psychiatry*, 1970, *127*, 652-658.

5
DIMENSIONS OF THE THERAPEUTIC SITUATION

The disparate characteristics of the child, the family, and the environment determine the dimensions and limitations of the therapeutic situation. As the therapist recognizes these limits, they challenge him to be creative and innovative.

Despite recent improvements in the delivery of mental health care, all children do not have equal access to therapy. The type of treatment, the characteristics of the therapist, and the time lapse between referral and treatment are often determined strictly by the location and financial status of the child's family.

Transportation, food, clothing, medical care, and housing are not critical considerations to a family with adequate resources, but to a family in marginal circumstances they are vital. It may be that therapy can be implemented only if the therapist can arrange for the child's transportation. Realistically, food, shelter, and clothing are higher on the family's list of priorities than psychiatric help for the child. Because a hungry child cannot make maximal use of therapy, innovation is called for. The therapist may either become discouraged or accept the challenge. Giving practical advice to the parents, or becoming their advocate in the welfare or medical system, may also be required before therapy can proceed.

Limitations

Physical disability or illness may impose limitations on the therapeutic situation. Mary, a child with sickle-cell anemia who had experienced several crises with severe pain, is an example. One of her friends had the same illness which resulted in cerebral thrombosis with temporary paralysis. Mary felt she lived with a "loaded gun" pointed at her head since she never knew when the disease would strike. The therapeutic task with Mary was to help her adapt to her anxiety-provoking illness.

A different situation was presented by Jane, whose leukemia had been in remission for several years. She was referred to a child psychiatrist for being "bossy" and rude. The evaluation of her family indicated that Jane's chronic illness was not the major determinant in her behavior. Jane's mother felt inadequate in her role. The family reported that Jane had seemed "bossy" long before the diagnosis of leukemia was made. Therapy was directed toward increasing the mother's confidence and helping Jane find more appropriate ways of interacting. When a child has a chronic illness, it cannot automatically be assumed that it is the primary cause of the emotional difficulty. Illness must not become a primary limitation in therapy.

A major physical or emotional illness in a parent is another component that influences the therapeutic situation. A parent with a major physical or mental handicap might require help in homemaking or child-rearing. The effects of the parent's limitations on the child must be explored in the therapy. One child was confused, frightened, and angry because he could not understand his mother's need for the long rest periods made necessary by her chronic illness. Since she appeared healthy to him, he interpreted her need for rest as "selfishness." The therapist was able to help him adapt to his mother who "was not like other mothers" who were healthy and vital.

CULTURAL DIFFERENCES: COMMUNICATING WITH THE FAMILY

The language used in the home can also influence therapy, as can cultural orientation and the system of belief, because the therapist and the family may speak the same words but not the same "language." Cultural orientation and differences also require close attention and understanding, as do belief systems, since they exert a strong influence on the course of therapy. A child, whose cultural milieu has significant elements of magic and the supernatural, may find it uncomfortable to work with the concepts that thinking and doing are not the same thing.

The composition of the child's immediate family is an important background variable. Not every child lives in a traditional, intact, nuclear family home. Some live in a variety of family settings, with living arrangements that influence his ideas of what a family is and should be. Because of their own backgrounds, therapists may have a strong bias about what constitutes the "best" family constellation for all children, not recognizing that there may be strengths in the family of a troubled child even if the family structure is nontraditional. This may not be the principal cause of the child's troubles. Rather, the important issue—which the therapist must comprehend—is the *meaning* of the family to the child. Transference, resistance, and other unconscious factors and problems will arise in therapy. Therefore, tactful discussion of the realistic aspects of therapy can minimize their effects. Though the therapist and parents will not discuss all elements of the relationship, the parents deserve to know what therapy will entail and how the therapist functions. Basic topics for discussion should include: confidentiality; financial arrangements; appointment scheduling; involvement of the parents in the therapeutic process; and anticipated length of treatment.

Sometimes parents are only too eager to have their child in therapy because of their guilt or their desire to have the therapist take on the responsibility for helping their troubled child. The clinician should be sensitive to parents who acquiesce to whatever is asked of them without question. It is natural for parents to ask questions that cannot be answered easily such as, "How long will it take?" and "What caused the problem?"

Conversely, the questions may indicate underlying guilt or resistance, another reason to discuss with parents the dimensions and limitations of therapy. The clinician can obtain clues from the interaction with the parents that will aid the therapy as it proceeds.

Because some children come for therapy at the request of the school, the parents may deny the problem and blame the school. When a family comes to the clinician under duress, this inevitably limits the initial phase of treatment. Eventually the parents' and child's resistance may diminish, or personal or marital problems motivate the family to continue. But if there is no progress in outpatient treatment, the therapist must consider alternatives such as day or residential treatment, or foster home placement.

PLAY THERAPY

Because children, compared to adults, are limited in their ability to communicate verbally, toys and other materials may be necessary. Play therapy is a generic term to describe one form of psychotherapeutic work with children. Thus, every article in the "playroom" must be selected for its therapeutic usefulness. Children quickly understand that this is quite different from their playroom or toys at home. Sometimes early in therapy they may even make disparaging or insightful remarks about the contrast. They seem to adapt quickly, however, and their use of play materials becomes an extension of their feelings and preoccupations.

The available materials should permit a wide range of fantasy play, emotional expression, and artistic creativeness. They must be appropriate to the child's chronological age, developmental stage, and physical and neurological status.

A shift in play materials is a useful maneuver that helps a child who feels threatened and who is overcome with anxiety. Materials have many different uses during these therapy sessions since they are more symbolic than "real." Even when ignored, they can reveal a great deal about the child's status.

The older child or adolescent requires a larger chair near the therapist's desk and materials for doodling or fidgeting, as well as more structured activity. Basic rules for the playroom are that the child can't hurt himself, can't hurt the therapist, and can't destroy the furnishings of the playroom. There is also usually a rule limiting time. The noise level may need to be kept within the range of tolerance because of other staff members. The therapist must also be comfortable in the setting or a therapeutic relationship will not develop. For example, a sandbox is a fine, creative, and symbolic playground only if the therapist is comfortable with the possibility of sand all over his office.

A low working table with scaled-down chairs is necessary. A low footstool permits the therapist to join the play on the floor, because the therapist should avoid physically towering over the child. A sink with running water and a counter are welcome additions in a playroom. Toys should be carefully chosen and restricted in number to avoid overstimulating a child. They should be small in size to invite the acting-out of fantasies and the use of metaphoric language rather than large toys which are more likely to suggest physical activity and exercise. The toys might be grouped into different categories which invite the child to express his conflicts about aggression, competitive strivings, fears of big or strange things, dependency needs, family interactions, and eliminative functions.

In clinics where playrooms are shared by different therapists, it is difficult to maintain order in the playroom. Whether the child helps the therapist clean up at the close of a session or the therapist does it is a matter of preference,

but it is important that it be done. If it is not, the next child
is either overstimulated by the confusion or insulted by being
presented with broken parts, empty, dried-up paint jars, and
puzzles with missing pieces. Children from disorganized families are especially vulnerable to an overstimulating, disor-
derly playroom. Reminders of other children from previous
hours should not confront the child as he enters the playroom
and he should not be influenced in the choice of toys or
conflicts he wishes to express.

Play therapy can sometimes be conducted outdoors, although it may result in recreation rather than therapy; however, positive interactions can occur in this setting. A therapist,
treating a seriously disturbed 12-year-old boy who was obese
and clumsy, asked the mother to bring the boy's bicycle to
the next session. The boy's inability to ride the bicycle seemed
related to his fear of taking both feet off the ground at the
same time. His fear was aggravated by his embarrassment at
being so ungainly. With interpretation and reassurance, as
well as physical support, he learned to ride his bicycle for the
first time.

NOTE-TAKING

Therapists differ widely in their opinions regarding note-
taking during sessions with children. Audio- or videotaping
sessions raise somewhat similar issues, although there is little
doubt that they record highly "retrievable data." Extreme
positions are that the therapist should always take notes about
"important" material, or that he should "never" take notes.
The "truth" lies somewhere in between and it is relative,
depending on the circumstances.

It is important that the therapist be aware of the effect of
activities such as note-taking on the treatment process. The
child can be asked how he feels about it. This question often
elicits a variety of responses from the child. There may be

fear that his parents or others will see confidential material, embarrassment at what the therapist might write, or anger that the therapist is more interested in the notes than in the child. Some children ask, "Why aren't you taking notes?", believing that it is an indication of interest by the therapist. Other children make attempts to say "important things" and judge the frequency of "important things" by how often the therapist makes a note. Children, who have been engaged in acting out "delinquent" activities, have often been in contact with authorities who took notes. From their past experiences, they often see the therapist as another authority who is only interested in the "facts" and not the person.

After the session is over, it may be of benefit to some children to ask them to write down what they remember as important. Comparing what the therapist thought was significant with what was important to the child can be enlightening to the therapist.

THE THERAPIST AS ROLE MODEL

The child looks to the therapist for guidance and wants to be like him. The child must feel that the therapist is accepting of both his feelings and his verbalization. One little boy of eight, who had been scolded by the teacher for using "dirty words" in class, told the therapist of the scolding but would not tell him what the words were which had so offended the teacher. When the therapist suggested, "You mean words like shit and piss?", the boy was very surprised that the therapist knew those words. The therapist asked the boy where he thought the therapist had learned the words and the boy replied, "A bad boy told them to you." While the therapist wishes the child to have the freedom to use such words in the playroom, it is important to convey to the child that there are boundaries between what he can do in the playroom and the outside world, such as the use of "dirty words."

Another dimension of the therapeutic situation is its duration. Many therapists feel that a time-limited treatment
plan encourages more intensive working on problems. Open-
ended therapy has as one of its goals some personality change
in the patient. If psychotherapy in the playroom is time-limited, the therapist is likely to have certain goals in mind for
each session and will pick toys or activities accordingly. In
open-ended play therapy, it is the child who takes the lead.

6

PHENOMENOLOGY, TRANSACTION, AND PROCESS

To understand the therapeutic process phenomena, we must be aware of the determinants of behavior or action. André Maurois, in his essay on illusion, said that every perception is an interpretation. The observer's personal, social, cultural, and national background forms his frame of reference and influences his interpretation and perception of events. The observer's viewpoint also implies a certain cognitive set or style, particularly in relation to thinking about cause and effect. It follows that phenomenology is also determined by the observer's concept of the treatment process. The point of view of the American therapist would differ from that of therapists in other parts of the world. A therapist in one culture might treat a child by burning his clothes to drive away evil spirits. We are aware of the wide range of therapeutic styles as determined by concepts of process and culture. However, the focus in this chapter will be on the frequently observed phenomena in American children and families. The general observations in this context are those with which most therapists concur when they observe children.

GENERAL CONSIDERATIONS

Behavior is multiply determined ("overdetermined") but all determinants are not of equal importance at any given time. A single act or behavior may have multiple meanings, and

the meanings of specific kinds of behavior will change during
therapy. Physical development, for instance, whether a child
is short or tall, thin or obese, can influence his behavior. A
child who is different, or feels he is very different from his
family or peers, may appear overtly unhappy or defiant.
Chronic physical illness or handicap, for example, fibrocystic
disease, orthopedic difficulties, heart disease, minimal cerebral dysfunction, cleft lip and palate, cerebral palsy, and
blood dyscrasias, will influence a child's perception of himself
and, therefore, his behavior. An awareness of age and sex,
and the significance of these appropriate developmental
milestones, are important in assessing behavior. Within a
broad range, the therapist expects a certain level of motor
development, cognitive skills, intellectual functions, defensive structures, capacity for object relationships, and coping
techniques, depending upon the patient's age. Absence, distortions, delay, or precocity in an area also influence the
phenomena seen. Environmental factors, including past and
present history, cultural influences, and socioeconomic class,
are equally significant influences of behavior in therapy.

The environment

Much has been written about the influence of class, culture,
racism, sexism, and socioeconomic factors in recent years. A
responsible therapist comprehends the influence of all these
things on his patient, as well as on himself. Economic
de–privation can cause a child to be undernourished or mal-
nourished. He may wish for food, toys, clothes, and so on.
A child suffering from economic deprivation will require the
physical necessities of life—food, shelter, and appropriate
clothes, as much as he may need therapy. A disadvantaged
child does not necessarily experience emotional deprivation
or environmental disorganization. The primary deprivation
can be a lack or paucity of the basic necessities for daily

existence. If a child is also emotionally deprived, his affect may be "poorly" developed, so that his range of emotional responses is limited, his cognitive functions delayed, and object relations impaired. A child from a disorganized environment may be very active in response to the lack of consistent environmental expectations. Overactivity can also be due to his need to be hyperalert in a dangerous environment, and to appear omnipotent in order to deny overwhelming fears. Linguistic facility and the ability to daydream or fantasize are often underdeveloped in the child who has experienced deprivation or disorganization. He may also have difficulty in expressing or defining affective states. For example, the emotions of "mad" and "sad" are difficult for him to differentiate between or define, since little help was offered to identify and express these feelings by the adults in his environment.

Just because a child is wealthy does not mean that he cannot be emotionally deprived. Conversely, a poor child, lacking material things, is not necessarily emotionally deprived. The "poor little rich girl or boy" is fact as well as fiction. Rich parents might pay little attention to the child. A child with many material advantages may be deprived of a wide variety of experiences if his family moves in a limited or narrow sphere and has few peripheral contacts. The child's experience can be limited to friends who are very similar in background, to adults who serve the family's needs, such as tradesmen, and to adults who work in the home. Television may serve as the major source of information about people and the world; however, this is not an adequate substitute for experience.

Culture

Cultural styles influence a child's responses in therapy. For example, thought and act are the same for a child reared in

a home where religious teachings equate them. Such a child
will find difficulty in expressing himself, since thinking and
doing, in his eyes, mean the same thing and certain thoughts
are forbidden. Religious influences may encourage or con-
done expressions similar to hysterical or hallucinatory phenomena. Wilking and Paoli[1] report that hallucinatory
experiences in children do not signify pathology in situations
where hallucinating is considered a normal or natural experience for the adults in the society, and the latter discuss
their hallucinations freely.

Stodolsky and Lesser[2] demonstrated that the cognitive
styles of Chinese, Jewish, Black, and Puerto Rican children
were influenced by their cultures, and that the same patterns
were followed by both the disadvantaged of these four groups
and middle-class children. However, all the cognitive functions were less developed, an observation the therapist should
consider when undertaking therapy with these children.
Usually, the therapist respects and understands cultural styles
and differences, and variation does not mean pathology.
When parents ask for help with a child, they are concerned
about the child's behavior and optimal development, not his
culture.

Intelligence

A child of limited intellectual capacity will have conflicts if
he is urged to perform beyond his capabilities. In this case,
the parents are frequently the source of the stress since they
are unhappy with a child of less-than-average intellect, and
the therapist must devote as much time to helping the parents
as the child. Often the child's response is rapid when the
parents change, since he is dependent on their views, both
positive and negative.

The emotions of a slow child are no different than those
of a child with higher intellectual capacity. He feels as deeply

as other children, and frequently can express himself easily and directly, even if his vocabulary and concepts are limited. In general, he develops a very positive relationship with the therapist when he views him as helpful. His feelings of frustration, unhappiness, and anger may appear with relative ease. His defenses are often less rigid, sophisticated, and crystallized. The therapist's language and concepts should be appropriate to the child's capacity to understand, irrespective of his chronological age. Explanations may have to be more concrete, with fewer abstractions. Also, the retarded child, just as any child, would require help with "real" problems, such as being called "queer" or "retard" by other children.

The child with superior intellectual endowment may have an excellent vocabulary and language skills, but these attributes do not accelerate his emotional maturation. His emotional needs coincide with his chronological age, not his intellectual capacities. His defenses can be influenced by his ability to speak well, and resistance in therapy may appear hypertrophied primarily through excessive verbalization, rationalization, and intellectualization. Moreover, a child's superior intellectual capacity may not be recognized in a family where intellectual skills are not considered of any great importance. The lack of recognition of "fit" can be as significant as in the family with a retarded child and, as with the retarded child, assistance for the family or work with the school will be required if the child is to be helped.

Sex roles

Until recently, traditional sex roles have been well-defined for both boys and girls. Boys were expected to be assertive, masterful, and independent, among other things. Girls were expected to please and be submissive. The stereotypes are undergoing modifications; however, the concept of gender identity as different from sex and all its connotations is important. A three-year-old girl or boy definitely knows his or her gender and this is acquired essentially from the parents' knowledge and acceptance of the child as a boy or girl. Pre-school boy and girl activities—playing house, cooking, build-ing, climbing, and so on—are similar, but the child of each sex has a definite identity. During latency, members of each sex create groups with those of the same sex. Children within the group have shared interests and fantasies but, equally important, they enjoy competition within the group and an individual sense of mastery and self-esteem. However, groups need not remain segregated on the basis of sex. In gym classes, boys and girls, under adult supervision, are on mixed teams in competitive games. Winning the game is more im-portant than the sex of the team members. However, out-of-school groups are most often formed on the basis of sex because of mimicry of the adult world. Children form groups based on how they view and interpret the adult world.

In years past, observers reported that male and female roles were more narrowly defined in working or lower so-cioeconomic classes. There were definite expectations within strict limits concerning the behavior of both boys and girls, but these appear to be changing. For example, the working class is now more accepting of boys with long hair. In the higher socioeconomic classes, a boy often had greater latitude in interests that were acceptable, but a girl's role was still narrowly defined. Now, there is a blending of roles, and differentiation is less often made on the basis of gender than of interests and ability.

A therapist should be aware of family expectations when a child expresses an interest that was traditionally a male or female choice in the past. Some parents may allow the child a wide range of choices but others will continue to encourage traditional roles. The therapist should not necessarily accept the status quo or expressed opinions and desires of the child's parents. He will try to see if the parents are able to accept a larger view of the world so that the child has freedom to choose from a number of vocations and professions. With greater frequency a woman can be a mail carrier, police officer, lawyer, doctor, or engineer. A man might be a nurse, social worker, child care worker, elementary school teacher, and share equally with the woman in the child-rearing and housekeeping tasks of the family. Less often the man will stay home exclusively and perform the tasks traditionally allotted to the woman. The preceding illustrations are only a few examples of the kinds of information the therapist should have in treating children, with the awareness that this knowledge is always subject to change.

INITIAL CONTACT

Parents

Before the therapist sees a child, someone must first decide that the child needs to be seen. The parents may ask for consultation or treatment, or the initial contact may be made by a professional representing an institution, such as the school, social agency, or court. How the initial contact occurs can provide some clues as to the parents' readiness to accept treatment for the child. Even if the parents initiate the contact, they may be under considerable coercion to do so. Perhaps the school authorities have threatened to expel the child if the parents do not seek help. Juvenile officers or relatives can, under some circumstances, insist that the parents have the child seen in consultation. We should not assume that the parents are requesting therapy because they believe the child needs therapy. They may or may not believe the child needs therapy and possibly they are correct in their assumption. Consequently, it is helpful to clarify how and under what circumstances the referral was made.

After the decision is made that the child should see a therapist, one of the parents usually makes the contact. In most instances this is the mother, since often it is the custom that she assumes initial responsibility when the child is ill or in difficulty. In today's climate, if the parents relate to one another as equals, either mother or father can call. However, tradition and custom both still exert a strong influence; in some socioeconomic or ethnic groups a father will call about his son, but rarely about his daughter.

The initial contact can be made by the father for many other reasons: Father is supportive of an anxious mother; he is subverting mother; mother is ill or out of the home; or the parents are in the midst of a divorce and father wishes to obtain custody of the children. Following a divorce, if the mother is given custody of the child, as is usually the case, and father wishes to obtain custody, he will call upon the therapist to support his petition in court. The custodial parent alone must consent to an evaluation. If litigation is involved, the therapist knows the other parent is an adversary, but if the family is intact, it is common practice for the therapist to ask how the other parent feels about the need for consultation, evaluation, or therapy. Perhaps, in the last analysis, what is most important is whether one or both parents appear for consultation and whether there is sufficient reason for the absence of one parent.

If only one parent appears for the first appointment, the therapist should inquire about the other's absence. The absent one may not have been told, or may be resistant to being involved, or could agree that the child requires help but does not think co-parental involvement is necessary. This can be due to lack of psychological sophistication rather than resistance or opposition. At times, a child's mother will appear with her own mother, mother-in-law, or a friend if she does not feel capable of meeting the situation alone. Once therapy has begun, the parents may bring the child late for appointments, "forget" appointments, or, as frequently happens, cancel appointments. Yet, they will insist that they want the child to continue in therapy. If therapy is to continue, the nonverbal aspects of acting-out on the part of parents will require discussion and clarification.

When the parents agree that the child is in need of help, the therapist should ascertain the parents' focal concerns. Again, they may or may not be correct in their belief. They might believe there is no problem, or that if there is a problem it is within the child, or they may question what their contribution is to the child's problem. If the child does, indeed, have difficulty and the parents deny it, he can be acting out their unconscious wishes. Through the process of identification, he will exhibit the same pathological behavior as the parents. It is difficult for them to see this as troublesome or unusual if it is egosyntonic with them, that is, if they consciously hold these views within themselves. In another instance, a child's symptoms can be due primarily to central nervous system damage or primary mental retardation. If the family is well integrated, the parents may still need assistance in managing the child at home and in school.

Parent and child

Observations made while the child is in the waiting room with the parents can be instructive. For example, the parents hover over the child, ignore him, or are overly concerned with being "good parents." The child might be passive and fearful or demanding and aggressive. A child who constantly opposes his parents might change as soon as the therapist appears by suddenly becoming compliant in order to give the appearance of being "good" and thus not needing to be in treatment. However, he can also see the therapist as an ally in what might be the child's version of reality-testing. A mother who is overly anxious and afraid of separations can transmit her anxiety nonverbally to the child so that he is afraid to leave her and go with the therapist. She might also say, "Where are you taking him?", in a frightened manner. However, most children will separate from their parents if approached in a tactful, reassuring manner.

Every child is anxious to some degree in any strange situation. A child does not know what to expect in the initial phases of therapy. He is brought by someone who indicates that the child has a problem. The strange situation and lack of knowledge about what will happen to him are anxiety-provoking. He might think that patients lie on a couch as they are so often depicted, or imagine that psychiatrists treat "crazy people," read minds, hypnotize patients, or have the power to lock them up. It is the role of the therapist to explain the setting and the manner of therapy. The child does not necessarily ask many questions, but he wonders about what will happen to him, whether he can trust the therapist, and if he can be counted on not to "tattle." The therapist's comments and explanations should be given. They are helpful in that the child sees he is being treated with respect and concern.

A fearful child may not manifest his anxiety but reply that he understands what the therapist is saying and may appear excessively polite. He will come willingly every hour, find it difficult to express his anxiety and anger, but end each hour with a "thank you." A child who is afraid to trust can say he does not want to come, but may not want to leave when the time is up because he comes to like the therapist and there are times when he does trust him. Another child might bring some object each time to the sessions and wish to spend the entire time talking about it to avoid revealing himself.

Communication

Two, possibly three, kinds of language are important in communicating and facilitating the process of therapy.

Verbal—spoken language is one. Nonverbal gestures and expressions (sometimes referred to as body language) make up the other. Written language concerns us less in therapy. Nonetheless, there are times when a child patient can say things best in a letter, a written story, a diary, or a drawing ("I can't tell you, but I can draw it.")

There are at least two different kinds of communications which we at times feel compelled to share—feelings and ideas. Dynamic psychotherapy requires that the patient share feelings and ideas with the therapist if the interpersonal relationship, the vehicle through which therapeutic changes occur, is to develop. Feelings and ideas may be consonant or dissonant with each other.

In the process of child psychotherapy, many ideas (ideation messages) are expressed verbally. Feeling messages may be communicated as well by facial expression and body gestures as by words. In the case of a child, the sharing of feelings often comes first before ideas become very meaningful to the patient. This is true in spite of the fact that it seems safer to share ideas than feelings. For example:

> Mike was a 12-year-old fifth grader with a long history of social and personal adjustment problems. His mother complained that he cried easily, often felt "sick," and had periods of extreme dependency upon her. He gave away possessions and allowed himself to be manipulated to win peer approval. The school said he did not have friends, but was teased, rejected, and used by his peers. His need for acceptance resulted in his "shadowing" his teachers sometimes, asking questions, and making inappropriate demands upon their time. Mike's intellectual ability as shown by the Wechsler Intelligence Scale for Children was in the superior range. His achievement levels were at mid fourth grade level in reading and spelling and beginning sixth grade level in mathematics.
>
> The parents had been separated five times during the

past three years and this resulted in several moves between
houses and apartments. Mike was the youngest of four
children. The father was store manager of a small business
and the mother was manager of a school cafeteria. His
father had a drinking problem and was abusive toward
both the mother and Mike in earlier years. Mike played
with younger boys, or with girls, but not with boys his own
age.

During the interview, Mike denied being aware of any
problems on his part. He said that other children called
him names and that he was the last one to get picked for
a team. He was resentful of questions about his five- and
six-year-old friends and responded that "they don't tell me
what to do." He refused to take any initiative on activities
in the office, though he kept looking at a board game.
When the therapist suggested they play a game, he responded positively, but it was clear that he had been afraid
to ask. He later asked the examiner for "ten pennies." At
the end of the session, he wanted to stay "just a little longer,"
or to have "just one more." When his mother was in the
room with Mike and the therapist, Mike talked "baby talk,"
something he did not do when his mother was not present.

The verbal expression of young children can be facilitated
by helping them to label the affect or name the act. With
children who speak poorly, it is especially important to be
alert to the nonverbal aspects of their communications to
avoid asking them to repeat something over and over again.

If the therapist enjoys sharing the child's pleasure, he con-
veys this to the child by facial expressions and voice inton-
ation-modulation. It has been observed that the more mature
child therapists seem to depend more on talking with children and less on the use of play materials. This need not
change the balance between feelings and ideas, both of which
are expressed whether therapy is primarily talking, or a blend
of playing and talking. The balance does change if the verbal

exchange stops, or if the "interaction" becomes simply playing together.

Understanding the patient's communication is vital to therapy, and the first step to understanding is observing and listening—observing the nonverbal behavior as well as listening to the verbal behavior. It is perhaps easier for most of us to do the former than the latter without interrupting communication. It is unusual for adults to give careful attention to children and not give advice. If a child is critical of the therapist, it is difficult not to be defensive in turn or not to speak from strength and talk the child down. A therapist can talk quietly or noisily shout a child down just as a parent can. The child understands this, and can accept it either as the way adults are or as the best he can expect from his station in life, or he can stop trying to communicate because it is obvious that the adult is not listening. The therapeutic listener has the goal of understanding and putting himself in the place of the speaker, rather than preparing a rebuttal.

For effective communication to take place, the child must understand some of the subtle meanings of the therapist's language. If one works with Spanish-speaking patients, one can learn to speak Spanish. Most of us will never become facile enough to conduct psychotherapy in a foreign language, but the effort to communicate in a patient's mother tongue would probably please the patient. It is important that the therapist try to use the appropriate words in speaking to a patient.

In a similar vein, the current slang expressions in vogue with teenagers can be learned, but it is important for the therapist to retain his adultness. Communicating with the adolescent patient is more effective if done without sacrificing empathy or understanding, while accepting true differences. If the fads of language and mannerisms current among teenagers are adopted, the therapist loses his potential for helping in the eyes of the teenager. The adult looks foolish; the teenager may distrust him as a phony or as attempting to intrude into his world.

> Mary was a fourteen-year-old with symptoms of anorexia nervosa and a nineteen-pound weight-loss during the two months prior to her hospitalization. Both parents were professionals, although her mother had not worked for several years. Mary had previously become acquainted with a psychiatrist during some family sessions, when he was treating an older sibling for depression and behavior problems. A psychiatric resident, who was assigned to do the psychiatric evaluation and probably begin psychotherapy with her, had great difficulty in establishing rapport and cooperation, and getting her to communicate. She gradually "clammed up" and finally refused to talk with him altogether. The psychiatrist known to the family agreed to begin family therapy sessions with the resident as co-therapist, but Mary refused to attend family sessions if the resident was going to be there. She was willing to attend family sessions with the senior psychiatrist, who also began individual psychotherapy with her. Treatment continued in this way for some time. After a few months Mary explained why she would not work with the psychiatric resident. She said that he came on the ward in blue jeans and sandals "trying to look cool." He later took her to his office where "the lights were low." He had a teddy bear in his office and asked her if she liked to cuddle a teddy bear. "He used a lot of teenage expressions and he didn't act anything like a doctor and I didn't like being alone in the office with him."

By continuing to observe and listen so that the nonverbal, as well as the verbal, communications are received from our patients, communication will be facilitated and the process of therapy enhanced.

THE CHILD—TRANSACTIONS AND PROCESS

It is possible for a child in the initial interview to be relatively verbal or nonverbal. A preschooler may be verbal only when he is engaged in an activity. His play is not only a form of communication through action but also a help in discharging anxiety through familiar action. Generally, the preschooler is expected to be active while talking, since he expresses himself through action and verbalization. In therapy, play activity can be a form of communication, a source of pleasure, or an aid in the child's need to master a task. Therefore, the therapist's interventions are determined by his understanding of the activity.

The six-to-10-year-old or latency child occasionally may have the same need for activity that the preschooler displays. He usually has a greater verbal facility than the preschooler; however, he may be afraid to talk and feels safer and more comfortable communicating through nonverbal means. While modeling or pounding on clay, he shows how he feels. He could do the same by shooting darts or knocking over dolls. The therapist, by tactful, encouraging phrases, can help him to shift action into verbal language. Some children express themselves well through drawings which then serve as a source for discussion of feelings. Any one child may exhibit a predominant "style" throughout therapy: one drawing and talking about feelings; another playing during part of the session and then talking; or another telling about recent activities and then talking about earlier events.

Not all aspects of a child's style or mode of expression are pathological or in the service of resistance. If a child has a capacity or function which has been gratifying or adaptive, he will prefer this mode in therapy. A boy may draw, build with blocks, or make a model during the session; a girl will do the same things, or play with dolls, knit, or sew. A boy will play with dolls until the latency years, if he is not afraid

of appearing like a girl. If he associates girls with passivity
and must deny his passive wishes, he will avoid playing with
dolls or any form of activity he believes to be passive. Though
many boys in this age group will not play with dolls in therapy,
some will express themselves through use of dolls often to
vent aggression, undo feelings of helplessness, and to fantasize being powerful and omnipotent. Boys and girls, when
they become comfortable in expressing feelings verbally, will
less often use ancillary materials in therapy.

Play and play materials are vehicles of expression for the
child. They aid the child in revealing himself and help the
therapist in understanding the troubled child. However, play
in therapy is a vehicle but not an end in itself. At times, going
for a walk is indicated and helpful. However, going for a
walk may be for the therapist's benefit, especially since the
therapist minimizes doing something, by words or acts, that
could be anti-therapeutic. He might seize the opportunity,
then or later, to discover what makes him uneasy with the
child. Some children need to be physically active or need to
prove they are capable before entering the therapist's office.
For example, one boy insisted on hitting a baseball several
times. After several successful attempts, he said, "Okay, let's
go in." He had to prove he could do something and after
demonstrating it, he felt comfortable and was then ready to
go into the therapist's office and work on what made him an
uneasy and troubled boy.

Abreaction and its limits

Some psychotherapists have thought that abreaction, expressing feelings and experiencing the accompanying affect,
was one of the primary goals of therapy. Some continue to
hold this belief. There are instances when expression of affect
leads to some understanding of the antecedents, but this is
not usually the case. During therapy, abreaction does occur

in addition to all the other processes of therapy, but it is not an end in itself in most treatment. In a benign therapeutic setting, children often feel free to express their anger and fears. A child who experiences strong inhibitions, because of a severe superego, prohibitions, or fears of retaliation, will experience relief if he can express the "forbidden" fears and anger. He learns that feelings are not "bad" in themselves but that some modes of expression might be, while others are not. Abreaction is not a goal, but rather a way of reaching a goal.

Preschoolers may throw or pound on dolls, shoot darts at a drawing of a face, say they hate their parents or wish the "baby was in the garbage can," and laugh with glee. The child will feel a sense of freedom but unless it is integrated with other aspects of therapy it is usually short-lived. Sometimes it is helpful for children to express, with the parents present, what was previously communicated to the therapist and thus to see that they are free to say or do what they felt was forbidden. The parents may need help in allowing the child to express thoughts and feelings. A four-year-old boy was able to tell the therapist he was angry and frightened of his father. With assurance, he agreed to allow the father in the room and tell him how he felt in the therapist's presence. When the father came in, the boy yelled at the therapist, "You tell him," and ran out. Following a period of encouragement and support by the father, the son was able to say what he felt, with the therapist's assistance. This maneuver resulted in greater benefit for both father and son than discussion only by the child and therapist.

A depressed child may be nonverbal or very active and aggressive to ward off the affect of depression. Few children tolerate long silences well. The therapist, who is accustomed to treating adults, may wish to remain silent, but this usually makes the child uncomfortable. The child's silence may indicate that he feels no one cares for him or that it is hopeless

to attempt to alter his circumstances. This usually requires
more activity on the therapist's part. He can ask questions,
show interest or concern, and attempt to engage the child in
conversation on any topic that is of interest to the child. The
child then may talk about his feelings of depression or loss
with much affect.

When a child is depressed for any reason, or has experienced the loss of a parent which he has not mourned, he may
express strong feelings of despair and frustration. In most
circumstances, it would be of temporary or partial benefit to
allow the abreaction to occur as an isolated phenomenon. If
there is no clarification or elaboration, it may become a rep-
etitious phenomenon in the service of defense. In this connection, it is important for the therapist to be clear about
setting limits. When the child expresses himself in a physical
manner that is potentially dangerous or destructive, it does
not help for him to be without limits. The therapist should
not be attacked, and furniture or the therapist's possessions
should not be broken. The child will be frightened if limits
are not set. At times, setting limits will include holding the
child so that he does not attack the therapist or injure himself.

Transference phenomena

Transference phenomena do occur in child therapy but the
manifestations are often less apparent than in adult therapy.
In most circumstances the child is living with his parents, the
original "significant others." Therefore, his feelings, wishes,
fantasies, and behavior are still directed toward them to a
large degree. Consequently, in many areas, the child is not
"retaining" the past, as an adult does in therapy, and then
transfering onto the therapist feelings about significant others from the past. The transference in child therapy will be
less clear and nuances may not be expressed in as much detail
as with adult patients.

Fragments of the transference can be intertwined with present-day reality. The child may not be able to verbalize transference feelings because he does not have the language to express his feelings, so that often he expresses the transference in behavior. If he is afraid of revealing thoughts and feelings to his parents, he can be silent with the therapist in the transference, or he might be very verbal, as he is with his parents, but out of fear still reveal little of himself. If he is hungry for his parents' approval but does not receive it, he might bring objects he has made or his report card to gain the therapist's approval. Anger with the parents can be manifest directly in the transference as anger with the therapist, or if reaction formation is a major defense, the child may be extremely cooperative and "good" as he is at home. If he desires gifts or wishes to take objects home, it could indicate a need to share, to cling to the therapist, to believe he is worthy of a gift or to fill a lonely void, among other reasons. There are several determinants to the child's behavior and transference is only one. For example, a child who has few toys because his family is poor may want a toy for the pleasure it will give him, and this is more important than the transference aspect of the behavior.

At times the transference is clearly recognized. A girl will act out her oedipal desires in a number of ways: through seductive behavior toward a male therapist; gifts; verbal or non-verbal appeals to be admired; and verbal expressions of a wish to marry the therapist. A boy will enact the oedipal triangle by competition, anger, or passive behavior toward a male therapist, with anger or passivity usually indicating castration fears. He may be seductive, or attempt to be "manly" toward a female therapist. If he is frightened of his oedipal wishes, he might show opposition or be passive, as he is with his mother or father. However, expressions of sexuality in the transference could indicate that the parents encourage sexual acting out, and the child is overstimulated since adequate controls are absent in the home.

The transference is often reflected in the child's wish that the therapist be a magical figure, that he be omnipotent and solve all his problems. Hence, in the transference, he will be disappointed with the therapist as he was with his parents when they did not magically solve problems in the past. In the child's eyes, an enthusiastic expectation can turn to anger and disappointment when the therapist fails. The child will want to stop therapy. This may be a clear transference phenomenon or be reinforced in reality if the parents are failing the child in the present.

The countertransference

Countertransference phenomena in the therapist are as meaningful and potent in therapy as transference phenomena in the child. The physical setting in which the therapist sees a child should be comfortable for both the child and therapist. If control of sound and noise is inadequate, conversations of others are overheard and privacy is lacking for child and therapist. Both will be uncomfortable. A therapist might think that the child "does not mind," or might disregard the child's need for privacy since the therapist is the adult in control. If the therapist has many objects that he treasures in his office, he can be concerned about the child's movements. If the therapist is too concerned about being liked, he might provide many toys, candy and cookies, frequently give "presents," and permit or ask the child to address him by his first name to demonstrate that they are friends and equals. This serves to confuse the child since they are not equal, though at different times from the child's point of view they may or may not be friendly to each other.

Over-identification with the child will lead the therapist to be excessively giving and permissive. When the therapist has difficulty with aggressive impulses, he will allow the child to become aggressive and vicariously enjoy the child's behavior as some parents do. Or, again, the therapist will inhibit an expression of aggression because he is uncomfortable when it happens. In attempting to hide his discomfort, he might say that he is not angry, or imply that his anger will lead to a dangerous situation. He may even resort to making the session as bland as possible as a means of diverting or minimizing the child's anger.

When a child senses that a therapist has particular needs, he may do the following: concentrate on them to please the therapist, play games or make models which the therapist likes, or bring in frequent evidence of "good" performance and behavior, if the therapist asks too often about the child's progress at home, at school, or with peers. A child will be aware of the therapist's needs if they become manifest as countertransference. The therapist's ego interests will be evident to the child, but these are not countertransference phenomena and need not intrude in the therapy hours. However, when the child makes observations and comments, he should be answered unambiguously.

The therapist's countertransference behavior may manifest itself in various ways toward the child's parents. A therapist who imagines all parents are "bad" might be very critical, aloof, or exceedingly friendly toward the parents. If he overidentifies with the child, wishes to rescue him, and sees the child's environment as harsher than it is, he will be excessively critical of the parents and undermine their positive attributes. His approach to them could become overly moral and judgmental. The need to rescue can lead the therapist to recommend placement of the child out of the home when it is not indicated. If he feels as a child in relationship to the parents, he may need to please them excessively and in so doing avoid critical areas of discussion. His need for the parents' approval makes this kind of behavior necessary. He might attempt to cajole, seduce, or coerce the child into "good" behavior to get the parents' approval; he might be too accommodating when it comes to changing appointments, canceling appointments, and in other ways seeking the parents' approval. A therapist who needs to please the parents will allow them to believe they are not involved in the child's difficulty, even in situations where they are, and permit them to be the sole reporters of the child's behavior, or be the recipients of advice on management from the therapist.

The therapist who has unresolved conflicts over aggressive or sadistic impulses and controls them by reaction formation will be too permissive with a child in therapy. He will avoid discussing and limiting behavior when it is necessary. When he needs affirmation of his competence to bolster his self-esteem and avoid narcissistic injury, he will often strive for rapid symptomatic "cures," and in so doing can gain his own approval as well as the approval of others. The therapist who cannot feel comfortable with ambiguity, or adopt a formulation which has some unexplained facets, will strive for closure and not be receptive to alternative explanations when they patently are more suitable. If the therapist believes he must always be available, does not take vacations, spends little time with his family, or is too "dedicated," he may be acting out of his fears of abandonment or the role of the idealized "good" parent. He might not enjoy pleasure because of superego prohibitions. Though the therapist engages in various maneuvers as part of the therapeutic process, he is very much a "real" person. The healthy part of the child cannot fail to observe this person and it serves a useful purpose.

The "interpersonal" relationship

The therapist's use of the relationship to help the child grow was emphasized by Frederick Allen.[3] The child perceives a hopeful, positive, supportive attitude and the relationship is employed to further emotional growth. The therapist serves as an auxiliary ego for the child, in addition to permitting a "corrective emotional experience" to occur within the therapeutic relationship. In this form of therapy, the therapist will explain his behavior in relationship to the child and voice his feelings about the child. The existential, here-and-now relationship is emphasized. However, in all forms of therapy daily events in the child's life are of importance. The birth of a sibling, death of a pet, accidents, illness, parental quarrels, moving to another house, arguing with a teacher are only a few examples of current happenings which might influence the observed phenomena in any one hour. When the relationship is relatively free of countertransference, the therapist can observe many aspects of the child's interpersonal and intrapsychic life.

The continuing interpersonal relationship and the style or manner in which transactions take place disclose many behavioral phenomena. To take a leaf from the transactional analysis terminology, a child who is not troubled would relate to the therapist in a child/adult manner. However, a disturbed child could be committed to an infant/adult or pseudo-adult/adult relationship. The therapist would expect a child with a strong character armor and highly structured defenses to behave in a highly predictable manner for a fairly long period of time.

The child has a limited range of defenses, but those he has are strong. They are also rather predictable and, in turn, exert a powerful influence on the personality and anticipated behavior. For example, where denial and projection are primary defenses, the child may: respond with a repetition of "No," "I don't know," or "I did not" to questions; be aloof and suspicious; or discharge anxiety by resorting to action. His need to mistrust all adults, including the therapist, will create a feeling of emotional distance in the therapist, since the child is attempting to maintain a wall to avoid closeness, with the possible pain that might bring if he feels disappointed or betrayed. He is compelled to maintain a stereotyped relationship. A child who has suffered from asserting himself, or who imagines assertion is equivalent to aggression, can maintain a passive role in the therapeutic relationship.

Coping, temperament, and defenses

Lois Murphy[4] stated that coping devices involve choices in ways of using one's resources and are also new structures and integrations developed by the child to master his individual problems with the environment. Defense mechanisms are often part of the overall coping effort and children exhibit individual patterns of response from infancy on. Individual differences occur in activity level, perception, response to stimuli, and "warming up" to new situations. Consequently, some of the coping behavior seen in therapy will be the result of a particular child's normal developmental pattern. Coping may be relatively conflict-free. Thomas[5] and his colleagues emphasized this in *Temperament and Behavior Disorders in Children*.

The therapist attempts to determine whether a coping technique is relatively free of conflict and appropriate to the patient's age, or used primarily in the service of defense. A child who denies dependency may not allow the therapist to help him with a task too difficult for him. He can say or attempt to show the therapist that he is capable of doing everything. Another child will have somatic symptoms, ranging from minimal complaints to severe psychosomatic symptoms, as regressive defensive maneuvers in the face of anxiety. Also, children frequently feel that, if they inhibit specific activities and do not admit their thoughts, then the thoughts will not exist. These are examples of magical thinking. Certain defense mechanisms are predominant at specific ages: denial and projection are frequent in the younger pre-school child but they are not primary in the normal latency child.

In place of the capacity for object relations, the child may use identification, such as identification with the aggressor. This is seen in therapy when the child must be all-powerful and in control. The need to be active is manifest when a child, fearful of being passive, adopts motor activity as a means of diminishing anxiety. Some children feign or feel boredom and say they are bored, when they are defending against becoming aware of unpleasant affects. Others will oppose the therapist to defend themselves from becoming aware of positive feelings toward him. This demonstrates how one drive—aggression—can be used as a defense against another—the libidinal. Some children who are aware of positive feelings will react by shyness or they will blush. As is often the case with children, defensive phenomena are seen in overt behavior, since so much of a child's daily existence involves action and a lessened ability to use language, as compared to adults.

The child's natural identification with a parent might be the cause of cyclic phenomena, since identification occurs in relationship to all aspects of the parent as a model. If a mother or father is prone to recurrent depressive cycles, the child may display this phenomenon, which can alternate with optimism. The identification can be part of the historical past or exist in the present. If a parent has recurrent anxiety and headaches, stomachaches, or vomiting that are manifestations of tension, it is possible for the child to have similar symptoms.

Preadolescent girls can become tense, somewhat irritable and argumentative, and more active several months before menarche. This is not a permanent cyclic phenomenon. It may occur during therapy and is not necessarily indicative

of an abnormal phenomenon, but is part of the normal process of maturation influenced by endocrine changes.

Memory, recall, and remembering

At times the therapist may observe recurrent or cyclical affective phenomena which are related to past events in the
child's life, or to the present. When repression of an event
has occurred, only the dissociated affect recurs. Anniversary
reactions, associated with a loss, and absent or incomplete
mourning can be the cause of recurrent affective cycles.
Other potentially traumatic past events that might undergo
repression and contribute to affective cycles are the birth of
a sibling, mother's serious illness with or without separation
from the child, past illnesses in the child, a sudden separation
with intense feelings of helplessness, and repressed sexual
fantasies or activities.

The process of recall or remembering during therapy is
subject to a number of forces; some are normal and others
are not. A three-year-old will recall several events occurring
from two-to-three years of age. As he grows older, the process
of infantile amnesia appears and most of the early memories
are beyond recall. The therapist would not expect the older
child to recall very early events. Like dreams, memories are
subject to amnesia, condensation, displacement, and secondary elaboration. For example, several surgical procedures can
be condensed or telescoped into one operation and displacement in time occurs, so that the operation or operations are
remembered as happening earlier or later than the actual
event.

Memory distortion depends on many elements: past and
present experiences, level of ego development, wishes, fantasies, and defenses, among others. Consequently, a child's
capacity to remember or not to remember is important, and
distortions in memory or elaborations and additions are sig-

nificant. Some children do not want to remember because it is too painful and anxiety-provoking; others must believe they remember every event from birth onward. Those who believe they remember everything often feel that one absent link in the chain of events leaves them in an existential void with its accompanying dread. One is impressed when a child shows a "hypertrophy" of memory, with a need to know everything as a defensive function. Simultaneously, there are difficulties in object relations so that a clear demarcation between self and object is blurred, as occurs in borderline characters, autism, or childhood schizophrenia.

Defensively, one child will remember the past as completely happy, and deny any frustrations or unhappiness. Another child may remember predominantly sad, tragic events, and these memories can be real if the caretakers were harsh and cruel. They may not be real but he is afraid to hope for anything pleasant for fear of disappointment since he has been hurt in the past.

During therapy, the availability of psychic material varies from child to child. In contrast to adults, children report dreams less frequently. When they are reported, associations are often very limited. The therapist should avoid making symbolic interpretations in most instances. Fantasies are often more available and with encouragement the child will talk about them, but some children will be embarrassed initially, since they know their desires are beyond their capacities for achievement. Embarrassment or worry may be evident if the child believes that fantasies about sex, aggression, and ambition are forbidden. This can occur when a child believes the thought equals the deed or when he believes he must always be "good." Repression can be so strong that he is not aware of fantasies. In this instance, the therapist attempts to serve as a benign permissive adult so that the child is free to remember.

Some children find it difficult to remember if their mem-

ories are painful and associated with much anxiety and
depression. For them it is more comfortable to live in the
present, but by their actions they do communicate what tran-
spired in the past. Some children have many accurate memories; others remember only selected events and repress
others, while still others will intersperse significant distortions
with more accurate memories. To some degree, all memories
are subject to some distortion, since recall is influenced by
the affect at the time of the event and by the present affective
state. When a child reports memories of events which happened too early for him to remember, he often has been told
about the events so frequently that he believes he remembers
them. Memories should be related to the total context of
therapy. Sometimes they will be more significant than other
aspects of the therapy, and at times they will not. Children,
in general, will not relate to a series of memories as well as
adults in therapy; thus, they can recall an event and elaborate
but usually will not free associate to a number of other memories.

Some children remember chiefly through play activities,
drawings, or behavior. Action is often split from ideation,
thought, or memory, and the therapist attempts to bridge
the gap through inquiry or interpretation. The child's symptomatic behavior may occur within the therapeutic setting,
at home, awake, or asleep. For instance, the child may be
subject to night terrors or somnambulism. These phenomena
may not be available to discussion in therapy for a long period
of time, since recall is so difficult. However, when behavior
is clearly a transference phenomenon, it is subject to interpretations. For example, when a child acts in a consistently
passive or aggressive manner because he fears the therapist,
he may respond to appropriate interpretation. If the interpretation is premature, there will be no change in behavior.
Conversely, if intervention is delayed, the behavior will per-

sist under the influence of the repetition compulsion. There-fore, as in all interpretations, timing and tact are crucial.

Verbal and nonverbal transactions

Verbal exchange between child and therapist is composed of many elements. The therapist says many things to the child and everything he says is not interpretation. If the therapist does not understand what the child is talking about, he should ask him to explain, and the child might be willing to do this. But again, he may show annoyance or anger, which can in-dicate that the child feels nobody understands him or listens to him. However, confused or unclear communication might be due to the child's need—in awareness—to omit or distort the message. The lack of clarity may be due to unconscious forces. If the child is afraid of the feelings but is unaware of this and cannot express himself, the therapist may observe associated movements such as tics, body movements indicat-ing uneasiness, stuttering, or stammering.

The therapist uses clarification, explanation, and educa-tion in addition to interpretation. Heinz Hartmann[6] empha-sized the importance of this in *Notes on the Reality Principle*. Explanation or education is necessary when a child should know some factual information, yet the absence of knowledge is not necessarily due to repression or distortions by the child. If the child is reared in a limited environment, he may not be exposed to the usual experiences, conversations, or events. However, he could have experienced or witnessed events but have an inaccurate perception of what occurred. Also, he may have been exposed to inaccurate or distorted explana-tions or behavior by his parents, but he accepts them as real-ity. These elements were emphasized by Hartmann. The therapist should attempt to correct by clarification. In this case, the child can be quite resistant, since it means he must admit that his parents were "wrong," and yet he is dependent on them. He will require a great deal of verbal support or encouragement from the therapist. Verbal encouragement is also appropriate if a child feels he is "never" going to succeed, or if he wants to attempt something and probably can succeed but is afraid to try.

Confrontations may be necessary when a child acts in a way to attack or harm himself, the therapist, or objects in the environment. At times, verbal prohibitions enunciated by the therapist will be sufficient; at other times, physical confrontation is necessary. The therapist, by words or acts, will show the child he will not permit him to harm himself or others. He can also tell him that he must be afraid or mistrusting. If the child has some control over himself, he may listen; however, if he does not attend to the therapist, the latter must act in the best interests of the child, though the latter may not appreciate it at the time.

Setting limits can extend from mild verbal prohibitions to placing the child in a restricted area, such as a "quiet room," if he is in a residential treatment setting. In times of tension or frustration, the therapist should remember that the unconscious wish or symbolic interpretations are of little or no value. These interpretations usually increase resistance and heighten anxiety. Interpretations are most helpful if made from the point of view of the defenses and not the drives. The child will show his readiness for an interpretation through conversation, play, or behavior, thus showing that material is preconscious and possibly acceptable to the child. When it appears that the child will accept an interpretation, it should be made with variations and elaborations on the original interpretation to clarify and make it acceptable to the child. He might show acceptance or rejection of it verbally or through his behavior. Though he can reject it verbally, his behavior may change in therapy or outside of the therapeutic situation and only later will he accept the interpretation verbally.

The number of combinations, variations, and permutations of phenomenology in child therapy is by no means limited to those discussed in this chapter. The therapist who allows himself to observe, imagine, and speculate will be interested and intrigued, if not fascinated, by the ever-changing pattern of phenomena in therapy which are open to exploration and tentative explanation.

References

1. Wilking, V. N. and Paoli, C. The hallucinatory experience: An attempt at a psychodynamic classification and reconsideration of its diagnostic significance. *Journal of the American Academy of Child Psychiatry*, 1966, *5*, 431-40.
2. Stodolsky, S. S. and Lesser, G. S. Learning patterns in the disadvantaged. *Harvard Educational Review*, 1967, *37*, 546-93.
3. Allen, F. L. *Positive Aspects of Child Psychiatry*. New York: Basic Books, 1962.
4. Murphy, L. B. *The Widening World of Childhood*. New York: Basic Books, 1962.
5. Thomas, A., Chess, S., and Birch, H. G. *Temperament and Behavior Disorders in Children*. New York: New York University Press, 1968.
6. Hartmann, H. Notes on the reality principle. *Psychoanalytic Study of the Child*, 1965, *2*, 31-53.

7

THE DEVELOPMENTAL STAGES

At each stage of the child's development, there are not only different and changing phenomena, but also differences in the capabilities of therapists to empathize with their patients. This demands new and changing roles for the healer in relation to children at different stages. Indeed, with progression up the developmental ladder, one must acknowledge the necessity for different kinds of healing skills.

When therapeutic intervention takes place at specific stages in the developmental process, the practitioner ought to be aware of the changing biological and psychosocial variables affecting the patient that influence the therapeutic process. These variables enable, as well as limit, treatment process in the maturing child. At least three factors can be identified to account for the necessity of a changing view of the therapeutic process as development proceeds: biological maturation; mental changes; and a widened social sphere for the child. Appropriate therapy demands careful intervention in only the most relevant sector, rather than in all sectors at once, e.g., the mother-infant unit, the family, the school, or any other setting.

The distinction made by the child between inner and outer reality is not the only event occurring during development. Structuralization of fantasies and stabilization of reality and moral judgments formed are taking place in interaction with the social surround. At the same time, the changing motor and cognitive organization of the child is taking place at varying stages of development. This makes possible an increase of independent action and autonomy, as well as intrapsychic structuring, which also have to be taken into account as part of the process of choosing the approprate sector for intervention.

BIRTH AND INFANCY

Biological lags may cause major difficulties in early infancy. However, even if the disorders stem from biological factors or disease, there is also a component of the mother-infant interaction and it is for this dual unit that the psychiatrist usually intervenes. Psychiatric intervention depends on the child psychiatrist's interaction with the pediatrician. The pediatrician decides whether a psychiatrist should be called in and, increasingly, finds there are child psychiatrists who are experts in the period of infancy.

At the initial stages of an infant's life, prematurity offers a child psychiatrist, as consultant, ethical and related problems in preparing the parent for special tasks ahead. A premature child who is kept alive and will have greater than a 50 percent chance of major deficits later in life requires an atmosphere that facilitates attachment after the baby is taken home. Attachment can be enhanced by group work with parents even while their babies are still in isolettes. A recent work by Minde and others[1] indicates that the attachment between baby and mother is quite disturbed in prematures, because the usual precursors to the birth of the baby are curtailed or absent. The mother who has not had a long enough time to experience her baby in utero has difficulty in approaching a child, a difficulty made worse by the devices for isolation, incubation, and monitoring used in hospital nurseries. Klaus and Kennel[2] examined the early bonding of mothers to their premature infants to determine the cause of the frequent battering of prematurely delivered infants.

The process of introducing the pediatrician to the idea that the psychiatrist can be helpful to him, the infants, and the pediatric nurses allows the child psychiatrist to enter into the therapeutic process. Whatever impact the child psychiatrist has on the child will be indirect; the therapy proceeds through work with the mother, pediatricians, and caretaking persons. All of these may help the mother make increased contact with her baby so that an attachment will have begun by the time the child is discharged. There are centers where, in order to make that transition easier, the mother lives with the child in a kind of half-way house within the hospital for a few days before returning home.

The mother-father unit has an essential influence on the mother-infant unit in these first stages. Any tension between the mother and father, possibly related to their diminished sexual contact or more likely related to changing their attitudes and self-concepts, may affect the child himself. Emphasis can be put on the biological state of the infant or on this psychosocial milieu. Thus, a three-month colic can be attributed to tension during the neonatal months or to the immaturity of the gastrointestinal system.

According to Green,[3] any extreme variance in mother-child interaction may produce infant abuse; infant neglect may also be observed in "failure to thrive" syndromes. A thorough examination of the mothers of abused infants often reveals that the mothers themselves have been maltreated. In the "failure to thrive" syndromes, the mothers seem to be empty, dependent personalities who need a great deal of nurturing themselves before they can perceive that they are not feeding their children sufficiently.[4] For example:

> Mrs. M. brought her malnourished three-month-old son, Thomas, to the pediatric clinic because of his vomiting. Admitted to the ward for dehydration, weight loss, and failure to thrive, the treatment process was begun with attempts to explore and to meet Mrs. M's own dependency

needs. She did not take much interest in Thomas, and
talked about her role as mother in terms of "my mother
told me." If pressed on the somewhat irregular nature of
Thomas' feeding, she defended her mother angrily—"she
always did that." It was clear that Mrs. M. resented others'
interest in Thomas and a low key beginning was made to
aid and abet Mrs. M.'s development, not as a mother but
as a child. As she responded to intervention, Thomas was
fed, played with, talked to, bathed, and reintroduced to his
mother, who, in turn, responded slowly to the tender loving
care offered to her.

Other syndromes, such as the regurgitation and ruminative
states and rocking or headbanging habits, seem to emerge
before self-conscious, self-reflective thought is possible. These
infants come to a therapist's attention thanks only to behavior
that disturbs others. Attempts are being made to intervene
in the distorted mothering process by bringing babies into
medical centers where they are given surrogate mothering
while the mothers are given training. In some instances there
is a radical diminution in the undesired, maladaptive behaviors. These maladaptive patterns are recognized widely as
reflecting problems in the mother-infant unit.

While the child is emerging from a nondifferentiated stage,
and moving toward one in which a relationship to the mother
will be established, the mother becomes the focal point of the
separation and individuation process. For therapists, the separation stage is best influenced by a therapeutic plan which
involves the mother. However, while it may not be feasible
or efficacious to educate her, the professional therapist must
understand the mother in her interaction with the baby and
try to help her, using techniques such as modeling. At times,
even interpretative interventions result in a gradually increasing awareness of the needs of and respect for the new
baby. The mother comes to treat the infant as an evolving
person rather than as an extension of maternal needs. Spitz[5]

contrasted emotionally neglected babies who almost died of marasmus with babies whose mothers treated the infants as narcissistic extensions. His findings suggest a broad course of action to influence the process of development. The child's therapist has to be careful not to lay too great an emphasis on the mother as an etiological agent or to reason too biologically about constitutional factors in the child.

The history of early infantile autism exemplifies how changing views of etiology influence therapeutic practice. Blaming the mother increases tension and decreases parental participation in the therapeutic process. With children who are born deformed from congenital or genetic defects, there are two people to consider—an overtly damaged child and a narcissistically injured, depressed mother.[6]

TODDLER YEARS

As the child enters his second year and begins to stand, walk, and speak, a new set of tasks emerges. Mahler and others[7] suggested that the child's growing independence provides a separate focus of will distinct from the mother's. Therapeutic intervention in these years may involve the well-individuated therapist's identifying with the toddler's insistent autonomy, while the unsure therapist may empathize with the mother, reacting harshly to the transient negativism of the child during this period. Toddlers may lead their parents into negativistic struggles which may become fixed patterns, with lasting impact on character. At the same time, a therapist has to be aware of the excesses of the "no" period and be able to empathize with the mother who may be dealing with a stubborn, defiant child.

Similarly, during the rapprochement phase, there may be an increase in clinging dependency and a tendency to return to mother at the level of a symbiotic regression. The child therapist must know the developmental landmarks of these specific phases since the mother may be working out her own problems concerning the individuation of her child. Any intervention has to reflect appreciation for what both the mother and the child are experiencing.

The father, if present and effective, becomes more important as the child's world widens. The father's criticism or acceptance of his spouse's characteristic ways of dealing with their child can have particularly telling effects. Some mothers tend to offer their child a good deal of freedom to explore the environment during the practicing or toddling period. Sometimes, the mother herself may have been too vigorously inhibited by her own overzealous and overcautious mother. At the same time, her husband may chide her for letting the child get too close to danger.

The toddler who is withdrawn and unable to relate because of an early infantile psychosis may be thought of as deaf by one of the parents who finds that an organic disability is easier to face frankly than a psychosis that could be sociogenic. Unless a child psychiatrist is called in and the appropriate diagnosis made, the therapeutic process cannot begin. When called, the child psychiatrist must balance the sharing of his working diagnosis in this serious situation with expressing appropriate optimism where the outcome is uncertain. In addition to these constraints, the larger social environment encroaches on the therapeutic process. There are some diagnoses which are more amenable to governmental help and societal support. And there is a moral demand that parents be informed. These are decisions a therapist will have to make by working with parents directly.

It is during early infancy, too, that sleep and eating disorders may resonate with the parents' own regressive difficulties that are derived from early interactions with their own parents. An important aspect of therapy and counseling with parents involves demonstrating that their fantasies and identifications are expressed in symbolic gestures toward their

children. The process is often educative and directive, because the family's circumstances will not permit a painstaking
process whereby conviction is built slowly. Frequently, the
process is best carried on the strength of ego support and
reliance on guidance, rather than developing insight.

NURSERY SCHOOL TO KINDERGARTEN YEARS

The three-, four-, and five-year-old child, ready for nursery
school and kindergarten, has developed to that point where
he can be socialized and even regimented. A more insistent
environment now demands that the child be placed away
from mother and family, and be at school and among peers.
His more advanced motor apparatus and cognitive awareness
permits the child to practice new social skills such as taking
turns and sharing. By preschool age, the process of therapy
may take place with the child as well as with the parent.
Seeing the child as the primary patient requires the therapist
to think about the variety of therapeutic interactions that may
ensue. Play is a medium with which children of this age group
are familiar, while talk explores a medium that they can
manage, but only for brief spans. One can always play *and*
talk with children.

Because the child remains emotionally dependent, the
therapist continues to consider the child and the parents.
This poses a problem for the therapist who now has to coordinate two separate sets of information, one derived from
the child and the other from the parents. Therapy must be
flexible and the therapist must be able to accommodate to
the child's shifting moods. Children of this age are exuberant
and lively, open and alluring, the favorites of many excellent
therapists.

The most difficult therapeutic question in the preschool
period is where to place one's therapeutic efforts. Counseling
of the mother and father may be an easy approach to prob-

lems, but if the child is blocked in one of the developmental
stages, therapeutic interest must naturally turn toward the
child. Tics, phobias, and obsessive disorders may appear and
require therapy during this period of childhood. There are
some who feel that this is an excellent time for family investigation or even environmental manipulation, which may include working with schools.

The therapist's matter-of-fact interest is important when
approaching a child at this stage of development. If there is
a tendency toward symbiotic clinging in the face of separation, the mother will clearly sabotage any separation unless
the therapist is certain of what he is doing and acts swiftly.
On the other hand, the problem of difficult separation may
be avoided right from the beginning. If the attachment between the parent and the child is too great, one must work
with the mother in the room. Exhibitionistic cravings and
reluctance about being seen at work may influence the therapist's judgment at this juncture. The parents' understand-
able feeling that they are being left out or that the child is
tattling can hamper individual therapy at this age. Parents
have a strong interest in their nurturing roles as well as an
interest in keeping the child dependent. Thus, the therapist
may appear as an intruder and can become the object of
parental hostility. Yet some mothers and fathers do not hes-
itate to use the therapist as a temporary babysitter and caretaker, thereby dumping the "problem relationship" rather
than tackling it.

The initial phase of treatment with young children may
appear *too easy* because there is something about their candor
that permits them to expose their problem rather early in
the process. But not unlike the adult hysteric who learns that
the therapist has some grasp of his defense mechanisms, the
child will change directions rather quickly. Once the child
gets interested in coming to therapy, he may have the mis-
taken idea that he is coming to play. And the mistake may

be compounded if there is not enough explaining and talking directed to the child during therapy sessions.

Therapists must be on the lookout for problems of motor incoordination, and of intellectual and perceptual lags. When there are perceptual-motor problems, they demand that more time and care be devoted to the process of separation from the parents and to the establishment of trust in the therapist. Moreover, the child may tolerate frustration and anxiety inconsistently, in which case one must swing with the child rather than stay in a cautious neutral mode. If verbal abilities are poor, play itself may become a defensive avoidance of contact. There is a temptation to manipulate the environment rather than take the time to follow the unfolding of the child's fantasy life. The oedipal constellation that antedates the latency period must be approached cautiously because the child must integrate the therapy with life at home. The therapist's vision is illuminated by parental reports as well as by the child's fantasy.

During these nursery years, there may be more desirable, and possibly superior, therapeutic modes than individual psychotherapy. For example, in severe developmental disorders, therapeutic nurseries may provide a more appropriate environment. They are sometimes coupled with triadic therapies (as in Mahler's approach) or with parallel mothers' groups—in which parental concern and the growing self-esteem of the child may be utilized simultaneously. This is a period not for group insight therapy but for semi-educational and therapeutic techniques that utilize peer relationships. There is a subtle connection between the mother's growing acceptance of her child and the child's capability to move ahead in therapy, as the following case example will illustrate:

> Shawn, a three-and-a-half-year-old, who was opposed to everything and slow in language development, was being seen in therapeutic ssessions with his mother parallel to his

involvement in a therapeutic nursery. His lowering looks
showed anger, although he seemed content when held between his mother's knees. Shawn himself was solidly built
and somewhat formidable in his silent watchfulness. The
therapist directed herself to the mother and the child as
separate units, overlooking the invitation to treat them as
one.

Mrs. F. intercepted words directed at Shawn and controlled the session with her own speech. The preoccupation
with control was obvious. Mrs. F. talked on and Shawn
remained silent; neither was happy. Then Shawn, who was
still half on his mother's lap, reached up to halt a flood of
words by putting a pacifier in her mouth. The therapist,
tactfully but repeatedly, pointed out that Mrs. F. and Shawn
were engaged in a struggle. Mrs. F. said she was afraid to
allow Shawn to stray too far from her because she feared
he might be injured. She was asked to speculate about other
reasons, and with encouragement Mrs. F. revealed fears
that she was not a competent mother; she resented the
demands Shawn made; she felt she had been neglected as
a child and had been reared in a very harsh, rigid fashion.
As Mrs. F. developed awareness of her conflicts, there was
less need to struggle with Shawn. In the process, mother
and child improved.

MIDDLE CHILDHOOD

Children of six-to-10 years have learned their parts as infants
and toddlers, have won through to latency, and have changed
imperceptibly their relationship to the adult world. The com-
pletion of certain biological systems have allowed their
emergence as small adults.[8] The change in the status of the
child between five and seven years of age has been recognized
in different ways: from *Now We Are Six*, the well-known children's story by A. A. Milne, to Cambodia's demand that children work for the public good at the age of six. Similar
recognition of "having arrived" is evident in Western cul-

ture's demand that the child go to school, and that he sometimes participate in productive work. The fantasies of a Christopher Robin and the enforced industry of a Cambodian child are transported into the treatment process, and the astute therapist acknowledges how cultu.al values impinge on children in middle childhood.

New skills, continuing growth, the exhilaration of doing, all reinforce the child's feeling that the physical self is competent. The autonomous functions of the ego are pleasurable. The child enjoys the ability to tolerate frustration and to postpone immediate satisfaction. Sharing and waiting permit gratification from school and peer group activities.

Although more reflective, school age children continue to act at times without thinking, reminiscent of their preceding adaptation level. Basic skills are elaborated and new levels of performance are secured. Verbalization improves and concrete thinking becomes less but, although thinking is logical in sequence, abstractions break down under the weight of concrete experience.

The improvement in fine motor controls allows certain children to be able to thread the rigging of model ships but others of the same age may struggle to hold and direct a pencil. Many are just learning the gross motor coordination necessary to ride a two-wheel bike while others have mastered batting a ball. The knowledgeable therapist, aware of these variations, will not make inappropriate demands during his sessions with any child.

The physical strength of a child is considerable. There are children who can throw chairs and accomplish even more strenuous feats; they can run and often do; they can hold movement in abeyance and sit still during therapy.

All of these skills may be used in the service of the treatment process. The therapist can point out the child's pleasure in self and the autonomous functions of the child's ego, and recognize the child's ability to work in treatment. Drawings at this age convey more nuances of feeling. Communication in treatment is enriched by work with dreams, associations, and play:

> In the first year in which Charlene was seen in treatment, she showed improvement with diminishing hyperactivity and anxiety. However, by the end of the year she was notably depressed and angry. Her previously easy response had given way to a pinched, disagreeable look and her voice was querulous. Her original therapist had to leave the clinic and over a period of time discussed Charlene's feelings. However, early in treatment with a new therapist she drew a cracked house with crooked windows inhabited by two neatly dressed witches, one older, one younger. Each of their brooms, at the ready in the closet, was discovered to have very small cracks. With time she was able to talk about her anger over the first therapist's leaving, her feelings of helplessness, and disappointment in adults.

For children in this age group, intense relationships within a small family group now evolve into less intense peer interaction. This bodes well for psychotherapy, too. The earlier fantasy play gives way to pleasurable structured games that require sharing, collaboration, cooperation, and competition. Guilt about specific feelings and behaviors becomes focused compared to the more diffuse feelings of guilt during the preschool years. Demands for absolute justice are made with considerable intensity. Their moral sense is uneven but, at times, children in this age group are capable of altruism. The following case illustrates a school-age child's continuing confusion caused by his preschool experiences:

> Kwame was viewed by his father, Mr. M., with whom he lived alone, as a very precocious seven-year-old. Kwame was abandoned by his mother when he was a baby. Mr. M. reported that she was let off "scot-free" by a woman judge.

This incident and its tremendous implications had not been discussed between father and son. Mr. M. said, "There are advantages and disadvantages to not having a mother." Kwame, when asked if his father could be mother and father as his father suggested, said, "No; maybe, sometimes." He said he had wondered about his mother with whom an older sister now lived: "I wondered what happened to her." In therapy Kwame had to deal with what is "impossible" to imagine, his mother's abusive, bizarre behavior, and the painful recognition of reality. He was abandoned by his mother who had encounters with the police, and he said, with much concern, "My father might go to jail," though his father had never been in difficulty. He revealed his confusion about the adult world, justice, and fear of abandonment.

The complexities of human behavior are perceived by children in the latency age group and one must take their awareness into account. Therapists should be cautious not to underestimate a child's comprehension of social interactions. For example, one boy of eight said, using a puppet, "The baby doesn't want to grow up in such a wild world," thereby combining evidence of cognitive ability, imagination, judgment, and logical thinking. The astute therapist hastened to acknowledge the child's sense of life's tragedy while considering the best way to undergird the child's strengths. The therapist needed to time properly any introduction of the child's reactions to his brother's violent death on the street.

The new skills achieved in middle childhood may obscure infantile sexuality. But sexuality can be inferred from the intensity and ambivalence of the child's interpersonal relationships. Drawings, projective techniques, and repetitive themes are helpful in exposing the continuance of early childhood lusts and images.

A full range of feelings is present in middle childhood. The adult does not always recognize the range, for adults tend to be preoccupied with the large-scale feelings of love, rage, and despair. But a wide range is there, from the child's gentle amusement and wonder through consternation and sadistic joy. The coping mechanisms are normally as diverse as the feelings coped with. Defense mechanisms, such as projection, introjection, repetition, and denial, familiar at any age, are used in rapid succession with and without embellishment *but* character structure is more evident at this age because of the child's tendency to use a more fixed array of defenses when adults are present. Latency children already show some of their character traits, a foreshadowing of their future stylistic adaptations:

> Carlo began treatment on a weekly basis with the understanding that he would do something—talk—and come to understand why he seemed somewhat sad and, in spite of good intelligence, seemed to get little from school. He slowly lost his initial interest in the treatment process after drawing too graphic a picture of a fantasied birthday party and began to describe to the therapist in stultifying, passionless detail his day, his entry into the classroom, his spelling words, etc. Verbatim reporting of these sessions was dutifully passed on to a supervisor by the therapist, who faithfully reflected the excruciating boredom of these sessions but was at first surprised to find that the medium was the message.

During treatment, the delicate balance between the need for dependence on and the need for independence from the adult is evident within the therapeutic relationship. This is an old theme to be dealt with, in reality and in fantasy, lest it promote too much competition between the therapist and family.

Children clarify situations by making use, in the treatment situation, of their skills in language, their understanding of nuances, and their gift for mimicry, while alternately turning toward and away from the adult involved in the treatment process. One seven-year-old, large for his age, being seen in the early stages of an emergency therapeutic intervention, cowered with fear in a corner when introduced to the policeman who came to take him to the precinct to wait for the Bureau of Child Welfare to act. Wasting little time on the specifics of the situation, he established his real fear: "What will happen, they will harass my mother." He later left with some bravado to see Spider Man on the precinct TV. When assured he did not have to act 10 years of age, he babbled "dadada" to the consternation of the police and social worker. Earlier on, in his ambivalence he had fallen back on the oldest of requests for interaction. "I know a secret and I won't tell." Treatment process for this child would have to begin by acknowledging the school-aged child's capacity to understand, tempered by his tendency to call upon more regressive modes of adaptation in response to stress.

The question remains of how to use the new attributes in therapy:

> Takim, an eight-and-a-half-year-old boy, was referred with the diagnosis of borderline personality organization. His mother was a fragile young woman, and his 10-year-old brother, who was seen in treatment as well, was in frank neurotic conflict over his father's absence and his mother's rejection of him.
>
> Takim, on a longer look, seemed to be a boy with some indications of central nervous system difficulties. Organic elements determined his difficulties in "hearing" and allowed him to put himself at a distance from others. He was concrete enough to say that the boy in the picture couldn't see the aeroplane drawn overhead, because he was "looking the other way." His mother said she loved him but couldn't understand him, whereas she understood his brother but didn't like him.
>
> In the treatment situation, Takim was responsive and

played in a somewhat immature fashion, with great pleasure, as a superbaby who flew through the air and rode a
tiger. There was nothing that was bizarre. He was comfortable as a younger child, accepting what his mother
could give. Continued treatment was predicated on
strengthening his sense of himself as capable in spite of
evidence of some minimal brain dysfunction.

Whatever the therapeutic process, and however maladaptive the pattern, these characteristics ought to be recognized
and enlisted for the good of the process, unless the child's
problems have made the development of one or more of
these accomplishments impossible. They are the stuff of individual treatment, of the therapeutic use of groups, of effective use of after-school activities and recreation, and of
the lessening of harm in placement of a child away from
home. Prior to deciding that individual therapy is required,
careful evaluation of the child's learning skills is also required. Too many youngsters of this age group carry undi-
agnosed learning disabilities that are burdens to their sense
of self-esteem. Those with frail egos will present themselves
mincingly, *or*, the other extreme, as braggarts to cover their
inabilities. Thus, the treatment process must involve not only
the child and his learning, but also the newly extended influence of school on his life.

The process of treatment is influenced by the age and stage
of middle childhood and further determined by the demands
of the individual child and his family, the emergence of new
clinical pictures, and the predilections of the therapist. As we
will read in Chapter 10, medication comes to be used more
frequently than during the toddler-to-kindergarten age
group, because of both the increased maturity of the child's
central nervous system and the inclination of the therapist.

Individual psychotherapy and work with the parents continue. Day hospitals and day programs, using the peer group

and the therapeutic milieu, continue the treatment process offered to younger persons in therapeutic nurseries. Specific family therapies can involve a child of this age realistically. Behavior therapies burgeon with the available structure of school. Psychoanalysis too can be tolerated by the child we have been describing. And for different reasons, periods of hospitalization are utilized for seriously disturbed children with varying diagnoses.

All of the characteristics of the latency age child can be counted on in preadolescence. Moreover, the child in late latency has usually become accustomed to peer love, especially for same-sex chums. That adds a special, new dimension to the therapy chosen and to the overall therapeutic enterprise with preadolescents, as will be seen in the next section.

ADOLESCENCE

The biopsychosocial characteristics of adolescence color the therapeutic process irrespective of the type of treatment in which teenagers are engaged. A brief recapitulation of biological and psychosocial development is helpful in this regard. *Normal Adolescence: Its Dynamics and Impact*,[9] for example, explores this topic in depth.

Biological changes

On the biological side, the adolescent has to adjust to rapid body growth, unevenness of growth rates within the peer group, and the maturation of the sexual organs and their functioning. Concomitantly, there is a rise in sexual and aggressive drives, as well as many concerns about the physical condition of the changing body. The "secular trend"—the tendency to earlier onset of puberty manifested in industrialized countries during this century—has compounded the emotional and social problems for young adolescents and their families. Four percent of American girls now experience their first menstrual period around age 10, while an equal number of girls do not begin to menstruate until age 16. Similarly wide, normal variations in the onset of physiological puberty hold true for boys. In other words, we are dealing with marked normal variations of puberty's onset in both boys and girls. Those variations influence all relationships of the adolescent, including the psychotherapeutic ones.

Psychosocial development

In the psychosocial area, the adolescent is struggling to attain emotional independence and a sense of identity in a society that often prolongs his dependence on family and the educational systems. The holding-off from adulthood may impede the development of the teenager's own individuality and sense of identity.

"I know who I am"[10] is often made difficult. The impersonal atmosphere of large high schools and society's contradictory attitudes toward adolescents do not help one's sense of individuality. Adult behavior is expected in some areas and dependent docility in others.

It is still useful, however, to conceptualize the psychosocial development of adolescence into four stages: the preadolescent, early, middle, and late phases as described in the writings of Peter Blos,[11] Helene Deutsch,[12] Erik Erikson,[13] and Kenneth Keniston.[14]

The preadolescent phase occurs just before the onset of biological puberty and is characterized by an intensification of sexual and aggressive drives and a reactivation of early childhood conflicts with authority figures. During this phase we usually see a recurrence of infantile (oral) characteristics (the egotistical, demanding, clinging preadolescent); toddler characteristics (the sloppy, stubborn, greedy preadolescent);

and preschooler (phallic-oedipal) traits (the expansive, show-ing-off, seductive, and competitive preadolescent). This is the time when girls may show the last thrust of tomboyish activity, when boys may remain hostile and belittling toward girls. For example:

> Jean was a 10½-year-old girl who was afraid of and angry with her mother after the birth of her brother six months earlier. In addition, her menarche had begun at age 10. Jean was angry and confused, and began to run away, dur-ing which time she engaged in sexual acting-out. In ther-apy, she was relatively nonverbal except in relating brief accounts of everyday activities. Sometimes she rubbed her eyes in a gesture used by a young child, when she spoke about a painful subject, and agreed that she wanted to understand what she was doing. She was a preadolescent who attempted to act as a mid-adolescent, and at times wore high heels and was very awkward. She could not restrain herself and continued to act out to the degree that resi-dential treatment became necessary.

Another salient feature of this phase is its very rapid growth of ego functions, sometimes called the phase of *second individuation*. This growth depends on the increasing stability of self-representations, resistance to regression, increased capability in verbal expression (rather than motor discharge), an increasingly realistic self-critical ego, and a move toward more abstraction. A conflict-free ego is allowed to expand its awareness of reality, secondary process thinking now be-comes evident, and a decreased dependence on the environ-ment to bolster one's self-esteem is evident. The increased distance from parents allows investment in others, particu-larly peers and peer groups. Self-concepts are modified by these peer group experiences. Clothing and appearance play a vital role in peer group acceptance and self-esteem. There is an increased awareness of oneself as a self-sustaining, self-governing individual. The superego, becoming less archaic and punitive, reaches adult form by age 14.

The next phase, *early adolescence*, coincides with advancing signs of pubertal development, the onset of menstrual periods, and the first emissions of semen. In the social area, the teenager begins to separate and pull away from his primary love "objects"—parents and other relatives. Close, often idealized friendships with members of the same sex are so common that some think this is a normal isophilic phase.

In *middle adolescence*, we see the "break for good" with childhood love objects, a separation that results in painful states of aloneness, feeling like a stranger amidst the family. The first experience of being in love often ends in painful disappointment. Self-preoccupation is further increased, and fantasies and daydreams are still more prevalent. The typical adolescent mood swings come to the forefront: one day an overevaluation of oneself, and the next, self-castigation. Frequent, grave concerns about one's physical condition and changes are seen.

Finally, with *late adolescence* or youth comes a period of consolidation, securing the sense of ego identity: "I am grown up," as an individual operating within a group. The sense of identity does not imply a discrete break with earlier life. On the contrary, it involves

> a sense of inner continuity and social sameness, which will bridge what he was as a child and what he is about to become, and will reconcile his conception of himself and his community's recognition of him.[15]

Now the young person is ready for intimacy in human relationships, for occupational stocktaking and choice, for constructive competition within society, and for social integration.

Cognitive development

In cognitive development, the adolescent after about age 11 enters the phase of formal or abstract operational thinking. Cognitive functions show a distinct shift from the concrete to more abstract levels. The capacity to argue logically, to deduce from inferences, to synthesize, and to form hypotheses increases dramatically. The adolescent can now conceptualize his own thoughts as well as those of others. He is on the threshold of freeing himself from some of the egocentric thinking of childhood. His sense of time is changing. He can see himself as a product of the past, and a part of the present, with an eye to the future.

As the adolescent grows, there remains much overevaluation of emotional experiences, in addition to a conviction that no one can understand how an adolescent thinks and feels. The young person's egocentric preoccupation with his own inner life is paralleled by the belief that others are as concerned about appearance and behavior as is the adolescent, and this may be a cause for suspicion and worry. Another cognitive development is the propensity to construct ideals and ideal persons, who usually prove to be disappointing because of their remote, unrealistic qualities. This capacity often leads to quarrels and confusing interaction, especially with adults. All these considerations help to explain the teenager's vulnerability to open or implied criticisms about himself—his proneness to be introspective, self-critical, depressed. The way he bristles up against adult hostile attitudes toward his chosen friends is just one example of this behavior.

Against this background, it is easy to see that the therapeutic process with adolescents, whether they are seen in individual, group, or family therapy, has to take into account their unique vulnerabilities and strengths due to their biophysiological changes, their psychosocial tasks and conflicts, and their cognitive strides. Any therapeutic endeavor with adolescents will be colored by the capricious, vacillating, physical stimuli originating from within the patient. These stimuli might be as dramatic as the first menstrual period or the first nocturnal emission, or as subtle as the first manifestations of acne, uneven breast growth, "growing pains," and associated hypochondriacal fears.

In the psychosocial area, often the greatest problem for the therapist is posed by the marked mood swings of the adolescent between depression and euphoria. Repeatedly, the therapist's planned attempt at "working through" a conflict with an adolescent is jeopardized by these unpredictable changes in mood. Clearly, some therapists cannot empathize with or adapt to this unpredictability and ambivalence. In addition, it becomes difficult to come up with a clear evaluation or interpretation, if their therapeutic impact is clouded by the adolescent's mood of the day: on the one day expressing an exhilarating, enthusiastic confirmation of the therapist's tentative suggestions, and on another day a negativistic, perhaps depressed rejection of anything the therapist says or does:

> Charles, a 14-year-old boy, had to return home from boarding school in an acute anxiety state. The necessity for Charles's return home was accepted by him and family but the precipitating factors were difficult to identify, although it seemed likely that Charles had been unable to stand up to competition in various areas at school, while maintaining defenses against the insecurity felt at home. While fighting off any real knowledge of himself or of feelings in general, he struggled "manfully" to win in an endless competition with father and brother.
>
> After several months of therapy in which he complained of the city, the subway, and the lack of intelligence all around him, he continued to resist the therapist's attempts

at clarification but made progress in relationships at home. He struck a final blow for independence by asking, just before the therapist began to discuss termination, if he could have a consultation "just to be sure he was not stuck with a lemon." Though Charles wanted relief from his symptoms, he was afraid of becoming submissive, which was expected in this phase of his development. However, he felt secure with the therapist, though he could not express his dependence. Through the relationship he developed a sense of integration and then terminated, which is not unusual for an adolescent.

In the transference situation, the adolescent patient may fluctuate between vehement rejection of the therapist, representing just another parental figure, and an easy, at times infatuated, acceptance of the therapist as an idealized, omniscient adult. So-called transference cures are never more striking nor more short-lived than in teenage patients. A special situation may arise between an adolescent patient and a therapist of the opposite sex when the patient becomes infatuated with the therapist. This sexualized transference frequently impedes therapeutic progress, and can cause stormy positive as well as negative transference reactions which, if they persist, sometimes require a change of therapist or therapeutic modality.

The strides that the adolescent makes in cognition also influence the therapeutic process. Therapy is often enhanced by the adolescent's ability to ponder and analyze his own thoughts, his past, his family and peer interactions, and his future. Therefore, exhilarating possibilities for engaging the adolescent in a therapeutic alliance transpire whenever the teenager's observing ego joins forces with the therapist. Granted, the moments or hours of engaging the teenager in reviewing himself critically and objectively with the therapist are often short, but these hours are rewarding and therapeutically productive. In family therapy sessions that include an adolescent, the parents may for the first time become aware of the cognitive gains of their adolescent son or daughter as they listen to his or her descriptions of family interactions. The parents often comment, "We had no idea that he could reason so maturely, objectively, and fairly."

The adolescent's recrudescent egocentrism, with his thoughts central to the entire universe, commonly impedes the therapeutic process and taxes the therapist's patience. The therapist who ventures to move the patient away from self-adulation or self-flagellation runs the risk of being criticized for showing too little respect for the teenager's "brain" and individuality. The teenager might become suspicious, hostile, depressed, and ready to sever the therapeutic ties which might, in turn, lead to a self-destructive mood of the adolescent, that of feeling isolated, lonely, and criticized.

A special but well-known situation related to the teenager's heightened awareness of his body, thinking, and family conflicts is the one of worrying about going "crazy." All the internal and external changes that engulf him make the adolescent susceptible to concerns not only about physical illness, but also about mental derangement. Over and over, the therapist has to recognize the likelihood of such concerns and help the patient look at the reason for such worries.

The adolescent in therapy is normally suspicious of any involvement of his family or school in the therapeutic situation. Especially during the early stage of therapy, even if the whole family is seen together, the adolescent often suspects that the therapist receives clandestine information about his behavior at home, in school, or with peers. A therapist who decides to work individually with an adolescent and *see the parents at other times* will usually fail to gain the adolescent's trust. Adolescents in individual therapy often accept the fact that their parents are seen by another therapist, alone or with a group of other parents. They are relieved to learn, furthermore, that after a while such parent groups tend to change their focus from the disturbed adolescent. In individual therapy the patient begins to trust his therapist and when the therapeutic alliance allows for reviews of the family situation, the adolescent often welcomes the opportunity for occasional joint sessions with his parents or other family members. This is highly variable and is dependent on the specific case involving the youth, family, and therapist; parents, on the other hand, can view this alliance as an attack on the existing family attitudes toward the adolescent. The following case demonstrates the need for flexibility in working with an adolescent and his family:

> Cochise was first seen in a family interview; he sat slightly separated from his father, an impressive Jamaican, and from his stepmother who agreed she was "a screamer." Three stepbrothers, six through nine years of age, welcomed an opportunity to remove themselves by sitting at a table and drawing strenuously. The same family group had been seen in the pediatric clinic the week before, after the little boys had asked their mother not to leave them with their half-brother. They described intermittent sex play with the two older boys over a two-year period, but never with the youngest.
>
> The family came to the child psychiatry clinic, agreeing that Cochise needed help, and that they wanted to be sure the little boys were "all right." The Children's Protective Services of Special Services for Children had been alerted and it had been suggested to the family that they had no choice. No one had discussed the usual procedures, rights, or the limits to family court involvement, and Cochise made it clear he had no idea what would happen on the first visit. The father had taken Cochise "away" one night, then decided he had no place to go, and they had returned home together. The father had not accepted the story in full but allowed that something might have happened. Cochise could not deal with the two-year history at all, except to say that no, he hadn't molested his two stepbrothers.

In the course of the one family session and two sessions with the father, while Cochise came weekly, the family made room for Cochise who had come from the West Indies for the first time at nine years of age just before his third and favorite half-brother was born. There was improvement in his relationship with his stepmother and vice versa. Mr. P. was encouraged to finally begin talking to Cochise about his mother's desertion of him at three months, Mr. P.'s removal to New York, and his and Mrs. P.'s wish to have Cochise with them instead of with his grandmother, with whom he had lived until he came to New York. Inroads were made on Cochise concerning his vast loneliness. However, his schoolwork fell off as, he told his father, he was "thinking too much."

In the eighth session with Cochise, he told of an incident which occurred on his way to the hospital which had great meaning to him. A young woman's dog had been hit by a car. The young woman got help for the dog. Cochise and the other bystanders urged the driver to leave, since Cochise said, "He didn't mean it, he wasn't guilty." The denial of guilt was repeated several times and taken up, without further acknowledgment from Cochise, in the next session. It was clear that Cochise was saying that he did mean to engage in sex play with his brothers, but it was too early for him to speak directly about it. In spite of this, with ongoing family and individual therapy, Cochise and his family continued to progress.

It is rewarding to most therapists to follow a young patient who is moving from the preadolescent phase into early and mid-adolescent life. In such a situation the therapist might overevaluate his therapeutic impact or success and underestimate nature's own healing process as the adolescent gets older. Probably more often than in any other age group, the adolescent patient sets his date for termination of treatment, or terminates treatment, when he has come close to breaking away from parental love bonds and experiences the first all-encompassing infatuation with a friend of the opposite sex. The adolescent feels truly in love and not needful of any more help from a "shrink."

The therapeutic process with adolescents can be singularly rewarding to the therapist. Keniston[16] has suggested that the positive emotional states of youth are characterized by a

> period of, at times, euphoric omnipotence, a sense that all things are possible, a feeling of utter freedom, limitless horizons and opportunities, a conviction that the self is malleable and can be shaped and bent in virtually any direction.

One wonders if these are not characteristics that have a particular appeal to those therapists who show an unwavering enthusiasm and patience in working with adolescents and youth. The therapist who continually attempts to stay abreast of his patient's fluid emotional and cognitive life greatly assists in delaying his own "calcification and Ivory Tower isolation."[17]

References

1. Minde, K., and others. Interactions of mothers and nurses with premature infants. *Canadian Medical Association Journal*, 1975, *111*, 741-745.
2. Klaus, M. H., and Kennel, H. H. (Eds.). *Maternal and Infant Bonding*. St. Louis: C. V. Mosby Co., 1976.
3. Green, A. H. A psychodynamic approach to the study and treatment of child-abusing parents. *Journal of the American Academy of Child Psychiatry*, 1976, *15* (3), 414-429.
4. Whitten, C. F., Pettit, M. G., and Fischhoff, J. Evidence that growth failure from maternal deprivation is secondary to undereating." *Journal of the American Medical Association*, 1969, *209* (11), 1675-1714.
5. Spitz, R. Hospitalism: An inquiry into the genesis of psychiatric

conditions in early childhood. *Psychoanalytic Study of the Child,* 1945, *1*, 53-74.

6. Green, M., and Solnit, A. Reactions to the threatened loss of a child: The vulnerable child syndrome. *Pediatrics,* 1964, *34,*

7. Mahler, M., Pine, F., and Bergmannn, A. *The Psychological Birth of the Human Infant.* New York: Basic Books, 1975.

8. Shapiro, T., and Perry, R. Latency revisited: The age $7 + -1$. *Psychoanalytic Study of the Child,* 1976, *31*, 79-105.

9. Group for the Advancement of Psychiatry. *Normal Adolescence: Its Dynamics and Impact.* New York: Mental Health Materials Center, 1968, p. 194.

10. Erikson, E. H. *Identity: Youth and Crisis.* New York: Norton, 1968, pp. 128-135.

11. Blos, P. *On Adolescence.* New York: Free Press, 1966.

12. Deutsch, H. *The Psychology of Women.* New York: Grune & Stratton, 1944.

13. See citation 10.

14. Keniston, K. Youth as a stage of life. In S. C. Feinstein, P. L. Giovacchini, and A. A. Miller (Eds.), *Adolescent Psychiatry.* Vol. 2. New York: Basic Books, 1971.

15. See citation 10.

16. See citation 14.

17. Meeks, J. E. *The Fragile Alliance: An Orientation to Outpatient Psychotherapy of the Adolescent.* Huntington, N.Y.: Krieger Publishing Co., 1975.

8

DYADIC PSYCHOTHERAPIES: THE THERAPEUTIC PROCESS

The end of successful treatment is marked by the child's new orientation to reality, either by adjusting to it as it is, or changing it for the better, if this is possible. In moving toward this more realistic outlook, the therapeutic process may be steeped at times in magical thinking, omnipotent ideation, and illusions regarding the nature of the therapeutic milieu and its boundaries. The deemphasis on factual reality is further strengthened by the invitation to the patient to bring in dreams and fantasies as an acceptable contribution to the therapeutic dialogue. Even the child patient soon begins to realize that this is not merely a doctor's office but a most unusual, enchanted place, where thoughts and impulses that are not considered permissible can be brought out into the open and dealt with as if they were part of the ordinary business of life. This in itself is extraordinary.

Illusion, in this sense, can become an important process in the service of therapy. It presupposes that normally concealed affects can now circulate freely within the four walls and receive the therapist's immediate consideration. It presupposes that almost anything goes within the time and place of therapy, and very soon a corollary to this may take form: that this is a place where internal unhappiness can undergo change for the better.

Milner[1] has compared this "therapeutic illusion" to the artistic one set up by the artist when he takes life as it is and, having distorted it in accordance with his own personal vision, places it "between frames" and invites the public's acceptance of any irreality he may wish to be present. According to Milner, the therapeutic situation is also set, as it were, "between frames" that gradually transform it into a setting in which the dream is made manifest, the past is drawn into the present, the wish is freely expressed, childhood memories are resuscitated, private thoughts are ventilated, and feelings are treated as communications from the inner world.

In the psychoanalytic situation, this illusional process helps to generate the transference, in itself an unrealistic development. When it begins to happen, the situation becomes tantamount to a "dream screen" onto which internal events are projected. By encapsulating the office and cutting it off from the "real" reality outside, the analyst furthers the illusional process. When the patient enters, he is implicitly expected to relinquish this real reality and concentrate all his attention on his psychic reality. When he leaves, the reverse is expected.

The office may look like any other office and contain the same office furniture, but the extraordinary atmosphere that is gradually created allows for the unconscious to be made conscious and for the closely guarded secret to be revealed. If the illusion is neglected and the situation becomes too realistic, the patient will assume a realistic posture and confine himself to reporting on the realities of his everyday life. The more realistic the therapist is during the early and middle part of his therapy, the more general information and reporting will be received from his child patients.

The illusional process is primarily the product of the dyadic therapeutic situation. It is difficult to maintain in treatments with families, groups or communities, and for this reason these therapies are much more reality- and goal-directed—less enchanted.

It must be borne in mind, however, that this process can be abused by both therapist and patient and create its own system of resistances. Since it is largely a product of symbiotic unity with all the regressive attractions of a symbiosis, the patient may become addicted to it and weaning may present a problem. The therapeutic situation then becomes a temporary escape from the difficulties of the child's internal and external life, and he may treat it as an oasis to which he comes without any intention of linking it up with the actuality of his existence. It is a place where he can "get away from it all." For the illusional process to succeed in therapy, it must end in disillusion. Enchantment gives way to disenchantment. The "frames" must be removed and the two realities must meet. The good therapist, like the good parent, may actually foster the unrealities of magical thinking, omnipotence, and narcissism during the early stages of the therapeutic development, and then, like a good parent, he will gradually introduce reality in doses acceptable to the patient.

THE THERAPEUTIC PROCESS

The therapeutic process is a complex phenomenon that manifests itself through the verbal and nonverbal interchanges between patient and therapist. It moves at a varying tempo through the session and appears to have a logical and chronological force that can be observed and described in various degrees of detail.

In 1940,[2] Erikson made an attempt to analyze the process under separate descriptive, impressionistic, and interpretative headings. He started with an objective commonsense description of what was being seen and heard, and then carried out a configurational analysis of what he called the "morphology" of the event in terms of temporal and spatial relationships—that is, where it begins, how it develops, and when it ends. Having examined the surface aspect of the process, he then proceeds to gain some impression of latent

possibilities, and to bring into awareness the classical mechanisms of defense.

Moreover, Erikson attempted to analyze process in terms
of space. He imagined a series of "worlds" enveloping the
patient and therapist, each with its own type of activity. The
innermost world deals with activities centering on the child's
own body (autocosmos), and next to it come the activities
relating to play with the play equipment (microcosmos) and
finally, beyond this, the area in which therapist and patient
generally interact (macrocosmos).

In the therapeutic situation, all these "worlds" may be,
from time to time, suffused with transference. Each develops
its own attractions and dangers, so that the child may move
from one to the other when he feels threatened. For example,
the emergence of "bad" feelings and impulses may provoke
"play disruption" in the microcosmos and bring about a flight
to the macrocosmos. At another time, the child may retreat
to the shelter of his own body (autocosmos) and become
oblivious to what is happening elsewhere. In assessing the
significance of these movements between "worlds," it is probably useful for the therapist to remain "fixed" himself, thus
allowing for physical space to be understood in psychodynamic terms.

Using Erikson's model as a basis for understanding the
process that takes place during dyadic therapies, we can describe a therapeutic session in terms of its processes on a
descriptive, impressionistic, and interpretative level: in terms
of the movement between "worlds"; in terms of the child's
use of different media of expression (play, water, drawings,
toys, and reported dreams and fantasies); in terms of the
flow of feelings; and in terms of the interpersonal exchanges
between therapist and patient.

In assessing the process during the course of the session,
it is important to determine whether it takes place in the
early, middle, or closing stages of the session, since time in-

fluences the process in many subtle and varied ways. The process may be slow and labored at the beginning of a session, accelerating during the middle phase and slowing down again toward the end.

At all times, the configuration of the therapeutic process is strongly influenced by interpersonal and transference developments. Untangling all these elements is not an easy task for the observing therapist, and he may very easily find himself lost between its various complexities, since feelings, movements, and verbalizations are all embedded in the same time and space matrix.

Apart from the movement between "worlds," there are movements that occur between the different media of expression. Thus, a child may offer a dream at the beginning of a session and then proceed to relate covert "associations" to it as he jumps from one activity to another: playing with the toy equipment, running to sand or water, modeling with clay, drawing, or dramatically acting out some theme. When he is "blocked" in one medium, he very quickly passes to another and continues his "associations."

Affects

The flow of affects is one of the most striking features of the therapeutic process in child psychotherapy. The therapist can observe, unless interpretations interfere, a positive and negative cycle of feelings running spontaneously throughout the session. For instance, strong positive feelings for the therapist may stimulate erotic urges toward him and movement toward the macrosphere. An attempt at contact and closeness may be rapidly followed by anxiety and panic, giving way to hostility and aggressive attack with the initiation of a negative cycle. The latter often begins with some direct attack, which then leads to retaliatory anxiety, guilt, remorse, an attempt at restitution, and possibly the initiation of a positive cycle of feelings. An interpretation of feelings may evoke symbolic activity or fantasy, which in turn often releases fresh affect. An interpretation of resistance, on the other hand, may bring about an immediate affective discharge which, if interpreted, may lead to the setting up of new defenses.

As the various aspects of process unwind, the therapist himself becomes increasingly aware of them and will in turn attempt to make them more conscious for the child. Toward the end of any particular session, he may review the sequence that has developed and thus provide the patient with a sense of the therapeutic process.

For beginners learning about process, it is often useful to tabulate some of these various elements as they occur during the course of a session. The concurrent use of videotapes helps to reinforce the therapeutic observations. And as a beginning therapist carries out his self-assessment, he will also develop the habit of recording his own responses during each movement and cycle, and thereby be able to assess his own contributions to the therapeutic process.

References

1. Milner, M. The Hands of the Living God. London: Hogarth Press, 1969.
2. Erikson, E.H. Studies in the interpretation of play. *Genetic Psychology*. Monographs. No. 22, 1940.

9
THE PROCESS OF BEHAVIOR THERAPY

Throughout history, there have been many attempts to control and modify human behavior by different means with reward and punishment in various forms as the basic tools. Although the term "behavior therapy" did not appear until 1932, or more specifically in 1958,[1] early application of conditioning principles to explain and change abnormal behavior was reported by Watson,[2] Burnham,[3] and Mateer.[4] The works of Shapiro and others,[5-12] Wolpe,[13] and Eysenck[14] created wider interest in the study and use of behavior therapy.

Yates[15] has given a comprehensive definition of behavior therapy:

> Behavior therapy is the attempt to utilize systematically that body of empirical and theoretical knowledge which has resulted in psychology and its closely related disciplines (physiology and neurophysiology) in order to explain the genesis and maintenance of abnormal patterns of behavior; and to apply that knowledge to the treatment and prevention of those abnormalities by means of controlled experimental studies of the single case, both descriptive and remedial.

Graziano[16] started with the more general term, "behavioral modification," and views behavior therapy as a subset. Behavior therapy is behavior modification applied in a clinical setting toward clinical goals. Most writers in the field emphasize the experimental base. Therapy involves an experimental approach to clinical problems, seen in behavior terms, in which relationships are specified. The general aim of behavior therapy is to help the child to replace maladaptive behaviors or symptoms with more appropriate and effective ways to meet his needs.

RESPONDENT AND OPERANT CONDITIONING

All forms of behavior therapy are derived from the foundations of the two basic types of conditioning: respondent and operant. Respondent conditioning, also called Pavlovian, classical, or type S, refers to the autonomic or reflexive responses which are controlled by prior stimuli rather than their consequences. This process involves pairing an unconditioned (or natural) stimulus (which is capable of eliciting a given physiological response) with a conditioned stimulus, which by itself would not elicit the response. Through close association, the conditioned stimulus gradually acquires the power to evoke the response without the presence of the unconditioned stimulus. A clinical situation involving this process is asthma, where attacks may be initiated by non-allergenic stimuli which have been closely associated with the initiation of wheezing.

The other basic type of conditioning is operant, also called Skinnerian, instrumental, or type R. In this paradigm, the individual "operates" on his environment to produce reinforcement. Conditioning involves the systematic use of consequences to shape desired behavior or eliminate undesired behavior.

The major thrust in present-day behavior therapy is in operant conditioning, and the emphasis is on behavior as it is controlled by its consequences, the reinforcers. Reinforcement schedules are of several types. *Random ratio reinforcement*, for example, winning when playing a slot machine, can be a powerful tool. *Interval reinforcement*—examples are accumulating stars for the performance of tasks, or receiving a paycheck on schedule—is not as powerful as random ratio reinforcement. In *fixed-ratio reinforcement*, the reward is received for each task. An example is a child who does his school work in order to watch television. The choice of reinforcers and schedule of reinforcement is important in behavior therapy, whether operant or respondent.

BIOFEEDBACK

An innovative therapeutic application of operant or instrumental conditioning is represented by biofeedback techniques. Children are said to be especially adept at learning quickly how to self-regulate some of their physiological functions by means of biofeedback, be it through measurements of muscle tension (electromyography), brain waves, or electrodermal activity. The impersonal technical aspects of biofeedback devices often appeal to the curious and literal minds of grade-school children and adolescents. They are challenged by the possibility of being able to control some of their bodily functions with the aid of gadgets.

In asthmatic children, skeletal muscle relaxation monitored by the subject via auditory or visual biofeedback has been shown to increase the pulmonary expiratory flow and reduce the number of asthma attacks, at least over short periods of time. Several recent reports suggest that electromyographic feedback training of hyperactive children may reduce their aimless motor behavior and increase their task attention.

An appealing feature of biofeedback as a therapeutic aid, especially in psychosomatic conditions of childhood such as asthma, migraine, and tension headaches, is its potential to increase the child's sense of autonomy and self-control. This learning of self-control over physiological functioning is primarily a cognitive, conscious process that leaves unexplored possible emotional conflicts and unconscious defensive operations which may contribute to the psychophysiological disorder. Consequently, the physiological "shaping" potentials of biofeedback therapeutic modalities frequently have to be combined with the more traditional psychodynamic techniques in order to engage a child in a truly comprehensive "psychosomatic" therapeutic process. Such a biopsychosocial approach is similar to the situation of a poorly controlled insulin-dependent diabetic child with attendant psychological problems; the therapist aims at engaging both the cognitive functions of his patient—especially as they relate to the illness and its management—and the emotions and psychological defenses of the patient in the process of psychotherapy. The diabetic condition often gives both patient and therapist a clear feedback of the effects of intrapsychic and environmental events which in turn can be "monitored" by appropriate psychotherapeutic intervention.

SHAPING, MODELING, AND ROLE-PLAYING

Only that behavior already in an individual's repertoire can be reinforced. *Shaping* is a technique used to create new behaviors. A goal is set and the individual's current functional level is determined in relation to this. By analysis, small steps are outlined to proceed from the current level to the goal to be pursued. Each step closer to the goal is followed by an accelerating consequence. The criteria for reinforcement are gradually raised until the goal is obtained. *Modeling* is another technique used to add new behaviors to the individual's repertoire. This has been particularly useful in assertiveness training with isolated and withdrawn children. Appropriate behavior can be modeled by parents or teachers as well as by the therapist, and rewards can be given by persons who share the child's natural environment. *Role playing*, either with the therapist or with a group, may also be useful.

The behavior therapist prefers that the variables be observable and replicable. The basic steps in planning a course of behavior therapy are: 1) a detailed objective description of the existing behavior and the desired behavior, and a determination of a baseline rate; 2) a careful analysis of the setting in which the behavior occurs or fails to occur and what actions from the environment precede and follow the behavior; and 3) determination of current consequences and choice of consequences to be used in changing the behavior.

The behavior therapist must understand or accept the tenet that, no matter how deviant the undesirable behavior, there is a reward to someone, the child or parents, from the behavior or it would not persist. A skillful analysis is required to identify what is maintaining the behavior. The choice of a definite goal is crucial for the success or failure of the therapeutic endeavor. It must be not only within the child's capabilities, but the program must be one that parents and teachers can carry out. Frequently the child is included in the planning of goals and in the choice of accelerating and decelerating consequences. The following example will illustrate this:

> Bobby was a four-year-old white male asthmatic whose coercive, demanding behavior was becoming an increasing problem for his parents, 31-year-old Mr. Tompkins and his 29-year-old wife. At intake, Mrs. Tompkins reported that Bobby threw eight to 10 severe tantrums a day, in response to parental refusal to meet his excessive demands for new toys, favorite foods, or the opportunity to go outside and play. (His asthma put restrictions on his outdoor play.) Bobby's tantrums consisted of flailing of the limbs, kicking, yelling, crying, throwing any objects in sight, and hitting his mother. Occasionally, he began to wheeze during a tantrum and required an immediate treatment to forestall a serious asthma attack. His parents reportedly had "tried everything" to handle Bobby's demands and tantrums, with little success. They disagreed concerning appropriate dis-

ciplinary procedures, with Mr. Tompkins taking a more
indulgent stance than his wife. Mr. Tompkins was a rigid,
obsessive-compulsive father with a history of anxiety problems, particularly with respect to health-related concerns.
Mrs. Tompkins was an aggressive, perfectionistic mother,
who was highly critical of both her husband and son, and
felt "boxed-in" by having to stay at home all day taking care
of a child with a chronic illness. Their marriage was characterized by excessive conflict, most of which was not
overtly expressed.

In approaching this case, the child behavior therapist first
conducted a comprehensive behavioral assessment of the
maladaptive responses, their current and historical antecedents, and their reinforcing and punishing environmental consequence.[17] Although the problem was presented by the
parents as a "child problem," the astute behavior therapist
recognized that the problem was a family interactional problem, also involving parental reactions to the child, the marriage, and the parents' individual personalities.[18] Looking at
the child's behavior, his maladaptive responses consisted of
coercive demands, excessive whining, and tantrums; the antecedents consisted of proximity to his parents, especially his
mother; the consequences of his behavior consisted of increased parental attention. Looking at the parents, their
maladaptive responses included their inconsistent discipline,
which was one example of their more general marital discord.
The following interactional sequence was initially targeted
for change:

1) mother and son are together in the home, the father is
   home but typically in the basement doing accounting
   work;
2) son makes an unreasonable demand;
3) mother refuses to meet the demand;

4) son begins whining, rapidly escalating to a tantrum, with wheezing;
5) mother is unable to control her son;
6) father, whose work is disturbed, comes upstairs, spanks the son and yells at his wife for being unable to control Bobby.

Following the procedures developed by Patterson and others[19] for coercive child behavior problems, the therapist taught the parents to punish tantrums and other demanding behavior and reinforce compatible behavior such as appropriate requests. First, the parents kept a baseline record of the frequency of demands and tantrums for one week; the mean daily number of tantrums was eight. Second, the parents punished each episode of demanding, whining, or tantruming by placing the child in "time out" immediately following the onset of the maladaptive behavior. "Time out," a common punishment used in child behavior therapy, consisted of isolating the child in a dull, boring location until he/she is quiet for five minutes. Third, the parents socially reinforced non-demanding behavior by praising Bobby for making appropriate requests at least once per hour. The therapist arranged for the parents to collaborate in a consistent fashion in the implementation of these techniques.

Over a period of five weeks, Bobby's demanding-tantrum behavior gradually decreased, with mean weekly frequencies averaging 4.4, 2.3, 0.87, 0, and 1.0. By the sixth week, the parents were spontaneously generalizing the use of the techniques to other behavior, such as Bobby's tendency to hit his baby brother. As the presenting problem was resolved, the therapist began to engage the parents in a discussion of their marital conflicts. It was felt that the marital problems would have to be resolved if the parents were to be consistent in managing Bobby's behavior in the future.

In summary, there were several key elements of the behavioral approach to this case which can be generalized to a variety of childhood behavior problems:

1) operationalize the presenting problem in terms of the maladaptive behavior of family members and environmental variables that maintain these behaviors;
2) teach the parents to observe the child's behavior as a way of assessing the outcome of intervention;
3) design an intervention to restructure family interactions by teaching parents to use appropriate contingency management techniques for consequating the child's behavior;
4) attend to variables such as marital conflict and personal problems which might undermine the parents' ability to implement behavioral change programs.

These procedures are germane to behavior problems of young children subsumed under the labels of conduct disorders, attentional deficit disorders, enuresis, and encopresis.

THERAPIST-PATIENT RELATIONSHIP

Some dynamically oriented therapists have been concerned with behavior therapy's apparent lack of attention to the therapist-patient relationship. Graziano,[20] in *Behavior Therapy in Children*, expressed concern about the tendency of behavior therapists, especially novices, to limit their focus too narrowly to overt behavior. He stated,

> Psychological therapy begins with a personal interactive social situation in which the generally expected human response of interest, sympathy, support, etc.—humane sensivity, in general—is the *minimum* condition, the *very least* to be expected of the therapist. This . . . must be preserved in behavior therapy.

He sees behavior therapy as starting with the basic therapeutic relationship and, only then, adding systematic objective strategies that are designed to have practical effects.
Reality problems and transference-countertransference issues arise in the patient-therapist relationship in behavior
modification as in all other types of therapy.

ETHICAL ISSUES

In considering the ethical issues in behavior therapy, many
writers have been concerned about control. This is a more
serious issue in the treatment of children than adults, since
children rarely come to treatment without being brought by
their parents. Treatment is also frequently requested by
teachers to improve the child's behavior in the classroom. It
is important to distinguish between the behavior therapy
used, for example, to eliminate a phobia where the child and
the therapist are working in partnership to remove something which makes the child uncomfortable, and that behavior therapy which may be used on groups of children in the
classroom, frequently without the children's knowledge, in
order to change their behavior for the *benefit of the adults in
the environment*. Those who advocate the use of behavior modification without the knowledge or consent of the child justify
their methods with their belief that all children benefit from
a more orderly environment. Winet and Winkler[21] disagree.
They fear that the use of behavior modification to produce
classrooms of "model children," who remain quietly in their
seats and do not speak unless spoken to, impedes learning
and perpetuates a rigid preoccupation with control for its
own sake.

Graziano[22] stated that all therapy is primarily a concen-
trated effort by one person to influence another. This is true
of all forms of therapy but behavior therapists are more open
about it. In our culture, contingency contracts, such as, "If

you take out the trash you may go to the movies," are acceptable and considered normal ways of child-rearing and
dealing with others. Any form of aversive technique, even
a threat which may not be carried out, is frequently considered negative, punishing, and restrictive.

London[23] and Goldiamond[24] addressed many of the complex ethical issues in behavior therapy. Symptom substitution
is the subject of heated debate. It is a common contention of
dynamically oriented therapists that the mere removal of a
symptom without correcting the underlying conflict will result in substituting another and possibly more harmful symptom. The behavior therapists claim otherwise. Blanchard and
Herson[25] addressed this issue specifically. If a symptom,
maintained by the secondary gain (social reinforcement) is
removed without providing the patient with another source
of gratification, a relapse or symptom substitution will be
inevitable. Hysterical neurosis would be thought typical of
this sort of disorder. On the other hand, a symptom that
results in decreasing anxiety and is maintained only because
of this decrease (for example, a phobic neurosis) may be
extinguished with little danger of symptom substitution. This
is demonstrated in the literature on behavioral treatment of
phobias, which documents the absence of symptom substitution or relapse. Blanchard and Herson outlined a three-
point program to prevent symptom substitution and/or relapse: 1) remove accelerating consequences to produce extinction of the symptom manifestation; 2) instruct the social
environment to reinforce positively all adaptive behavior and
to ignore symptomatic behavior; and 3) teach the individual
new skills for receiving support and attention from the environment in more appropriate ways. In the treatment of
children, the parents' or teachers' ability to ignore often dramatic and provocative symptoms, while positively reinforcing
more adaptive behavior, is a crucial factor, as the following
case will illustrate.

Charles was a 10-year-old boy, living with his parents and his eight-year-old brother, John, in a suburban area. Charles's mother, a registered nurse, called the child psychiatrist to request an evaluation. She complained that Charles was lazy and had no interests except reading. He was prone to hysterical temper tantrums which frightened the family. No means of punishment seemed to influence him. He seemed unable to make up his mind when offered choices, and had no friends. He was enuretic at night and had frequent stomachaches. Both Charles and his brother had been adopted. In taking the history, the child psychiatrist found that Charles had, from infancy, been an unpredictable, moody child with intense, predominantly negative reactions. He woke up in the morning in a bad mood and frequently cried and stomped his feet when he did not get his own way. Close questioning disclosed that he had never hurt or threatened to hurt himself or anyone else. Although he occasionally threw objects, he had never broken anything. He complained constantly that his younger brother was favored. Both parents spent a great deal of time trying to explain to Charles that they loved both boys the same, and demonstrating to him that things were exactly equal. In fact, John was a much easier child to be with and had interests similar to the father's, which encouraged their spending more time together. Each time the parents attempted to enforce a rule with Charles, endless arguing would ensue, and often parents would give in rather than precipitate a tantrum. Charles enjoyed school and performed well academically. Each parent had had some psychological difficulties with which they were actively dealing. This seemed to make them overconcerned that they be "good parents" and that both children be happy and calm. Charles reported that, in fact, he did have some friends. He was quite pleasant and verbal, although he firmly denied that he had any problems.

An agreement was made with Charles and his parents

to see the three of them for eight sessions to work on specific behavioral management of Charles's difficulties at
home. The most pressing issues seemed to be Charles's
tantrums and his constant complaining. The child psychiatrist identified these as negative, attention-seeking behaviors and developed a program with Charles and his parents,
which included practice in talking calmly about areas of
disagreement and parental ignoring of chronic complaining and tantrums. If Charles began a tantrum, he was to
be sent to his room for a "time-out" until he could control
himself. During the following week's session, the family
reported that Charles had not had a single tantrum and
that chronic complaining had decreased dramatically in
frequency and duration. Similar progress continued over
the course of the treatment. Parents and Charles negotiated
other areas as well, including a regular allowance and a
routine for Charles cleaning up his room without parental
nagging. Therapy was successfully concluded with Charles
and his parents feeling in much better control and happier
as a family.

Bandura[26] stated that symptom substitution will occur if
the major controlling condition of the deviant behavior is not
changed and/or if the deviant behavior is removed by aversive
techniques only. The questions regarding symptom substitution have not been resolved.

Many therapists in both the behavioral and psychodynamic
camps have seen behavior therapy and more traditional
methods of therapy as diametrically opposed. This is not
necessarily true. It would appear that the best course of action
is a detailed and sensitive evaluation of the child and his
family, followed by a decision to use one or more therapeutic
techniques, determined by the strengths and needs of the
child and his family, not by the training or preference of the
therapist:

Judy, an 11-year-old, living with her parents and five siblings, was referred to a child psychiatrist for treatment of irritability, poor compliance with parental expectations at home, and a habit of picking at her clothing until she had torn large holes in it. Judy had been diagnosed as having severe learning disabilities, with a verbal IQ score of 86 and a performance score of 60. She had been placed the previous year in a private school specializing in the education of children with such disabilities. Judy's parents were well educated, oriented towards high achievement, and valued highly family closeness. Judy had had muscular, coordination, and learning problems since infancy, and her parents alternated between overly high and inappropriately low expectations for her behavior. The mother felt that all the children should be treated "fairly" which, unfortunately for Judy, meant equally. It seemed that the only way Judy could compete with her siblings for attention was through negative behavior. Her parents' guilt at having a defective child and their uncertainty in expectations encouraged the persistence of this behavior.

One problem of particular concern for the parents was Judy's intermittent daytime enuresis. She had been toilet trained for years and was quite capable of remaining dry at school. However, while playing outdoors, she did not take time out to use the bathroom and the consequence was that she wet herself. In the face of this obvious evidence, she denied that it had happened when confronted with the fact by her mother. The child psychiatrist obtained a detailed history of the symptom, ascertaining that Judy was physically able to control her bladder. A behavioral program was recommended to the parents, including a chart to record the frequency of wetting and specified rewards for remaining dry. The parents resisted doing this for a considerable period of time because they felt it was "bribery" and "unfair to the other children." Finally, in desperation, the mother instituted the recommended program with the reward of a candy bar for seven consecutive dry days. Judy's enuresis ceased immediately and there were no accidents for the following three weeks. After this period of success, the mother could no longer withstand the other children's complaints that Judy received a reward for doing something which the rest of them did as a matter of course, that is, using the bathroom appropriately. This forced the mother to discontinue the reward program. Fortunately, by this time the behavior had stabilized and Judy did not resume her wetting. The child psychiatrist continued to work with Judy and her parents on other issues. Psychotherapy with Judy and her parents did not preclude utilization of a behavior modification program with success, and the program did not hinder the psychotherapy.

The therapist must at all times be aware of his theoretical preferences during the evaluation process, and be able to obtain a consultation or make a referral when the needs of a child and family are outside his areas of interest and expertise.

References

1. Lazarus, A. A. New methods in psychotherapy. *South African Medical Journal*, 1958, *33*, 660-663.
2. Watson, J. B. Behaviorism and the concept of mental disease. *Journal of Philosophical Psychological Scientific Methodology*, 1916, *13*, 587-597.
3. Burnham, W. H. Mental hygiene and the conditioned reflex. *Pediatric Seminar*, 1917, *24*, 449-488.
4. Mateer, F. *Child Behavior: A Critical and Experimental Study of Young Children by the Method of Conditioned Reflexes.* Boston: Badger, 1917.
5. Shapiro, M. B. A method of measuring psychological changes specific to the individual psychiatric patient. *British Journal of Medical Psychology*, 1961, *34*, 255-262
6. Shapiro, M. B., and Nelson, E. H. An investigation of an abnormality of cognitive functioning in a co-operative young psy-

chotic: An example of the application of experimental method to the single case. *Journal of Clinical Psychology*, 1955, *11*, 344-351.

7. Shapiro, M. B., and Ravenette, A. T. A preliminary experiment of paranoid delusions. *Journal of Mental Science*, 1959, *105*, 295-312.

8. Shapiro, M. B. A method of measuring psychological changes specific to the individual psychiatric patient. *British Journal of Medical Psychology*, 1961, *34*, 151-155.

9. Shapiro, M. B. The single case in fundamental clinical psychological research. *British Journal of Medical Psychology*, 1961, *34*, 255-262.

10. Shapiro, M. B. Clinical approach to fundamental research with special reference to the study of the single patient. In P. Sainsbury and N. Kreitman (Eds.), *Methods of Psychiatric Research*. London: Oxford University Press, 1963, pp. 123-149.

11. Shapiro, M. B., Marks, I. M., and Fox, B. A therapeutic experiment on phobic and affective symptoms in an individual psychiatric patient. *British Journal of Social and Clinical Psychology*, 1963, *2* (2), 81-93.

12. Shapiro, M. B. The single case in clinical psychological research. *Journal of General Psychology*, 1966, *74*, 3-23.

13. Wolpe, J. *Psychotherapy by Reciprocal Inhibition*. Stanford: Stanrd University Press, 1958.

14. Eysenck, H. J. *Behavior Therapy and the Neuroses*. London: Pergamon Press, 1960.

15. Yates, A. J. *Behavior Therapy*. New York: John Wiley, 1971.

16. Graziano, A. *Behavior Therapy in Children*. Chicago; Aldine, 1975.

17. Haynes, S. N. *Principles of Behavioral Assessment*. New York: Gardner Press, 1978.

18. Patterson, G. R. A performance theory for coercive family interaction. In R. B. Cairns (Ed.), *The Analysis of Social Interactions: Methods, Issues, and Illustrations*. Hillsdale, N.J.: Lawrence Erlbaum, 1979.

19. Patterson, G. R., Reid, J. B., Jones, R. R., and Conger, R. E. A social learning approach to family intervention. In *Families with Aggressive Children*. Vol. 1. Eugene, Oreg.: Castalia, 1975.

20. See citation 16.
21. Winet, R. A., and Winkler, R. C. Current behavior modification in the classroom: Be still, be quiet, be docile. *Journal of Applied Behavior Analysis*, 1972, *5*, 499-504.
22. See citation 16.
23. London, P. *Behavioral Control.* New York: Harper and Row, 1969.
24. Goldiamond, I. Toward a constructional approach to social problems: Ethical and constitutional issues raised by applied behavior analysis. *Behaviorism*, 1974, *2* (1), 1-84.
25. Blanchard, E., and Herson, M. Behavioral treatment of hysterical neurosis: Symptom substitutes and symptom return reconsidered. *Psychiatry*, 1976, *39*, 118-129.
26. Bandura, A. *Principles of Behavior Modification.* New York: Holt, Rinehart, and Winston, 1969.

10
PSYCHOPHARMACOLOGY

An increasing number of effective pharmacologic agents for the modulation of disturbed behavior have become available to adults since the mid-1940s. However, there has been a general reluctance to use such agents for children unless their effectiveness is well established by prolonged use with adults. This cautious use of drugs in children is thought to be prejudicial for both positive and negative reasons. One view is that of the practitioners who believe drugs are categorically inappropriate for children. It can also be argued that it is ethically reprehensible to prolong suffering and withhold a potentially powerful therapy from patients, when help may be at hand. Among the good reasons for caution is that children are different from adults in a number of ways that can alter the process and effectiveness of pharmacologic therapy. These differences require careful prior investigation of drugs in immature individuals rather than extrapolation of results from adults to children.

THE MEANING OF MEDICATION

The decision to use a pharmacologic agent is but the first step in its effective use. Inadequacy of patient preparation, inappropriate doses, or insufficient attention to process can spoil the therapeutic effect of even the best and most potent agent. Effective administration entails a complex process that includes multiple participants, amidst a mass of values and prejudices that extend outward from the child through his family, and ultimately to the community itself. Clinicians must carefully assess the context of drug use, eschewing a too narrow regard for the meaning of the drug itself to the child and family. The placebo, therapeutic, and side effects that the agent has on the child and his equilibrium in family and community must be weighed as well.

Starting with the individual child, our first concern is, narrowly, the child himself. The process of accepting a foreign agent, usually one that is ingested, is fraught with many meanings that resonate and amplify, and conjures up visions of required or forced feeding. The child's interpretation of the event may range from a "loving feeding," demonstrating care and concern, to a poisonous pollution of his natural systems. In preparing a child to accept medication, it would be well for the dispensing therapist to explore some of the more idiosyncratic meanings that will later aid our understanding of what may or may not be a pharmacologic response. Moreover, the placebo effect, itself, becomes a most helpful ally in the medication of some suggestible children.

PREPARATION

Careful but not excessive explanation of potential drug effect may prepare the ground for a child and parent. The physician must remember that, regardless of his intended rationality, parents and families have been taking some kind of medication for a long time, and old myths persist to color the new drug experience. Indeed the word "drug" itself may constitute a taboo, just as fear of prior allergy or distrust of physical agents for psychic ills may determine the outcome of such therapy. Popular ideas, such as more medication when feeling worse, may have to be undone by explaining how the medicine works, takes hold, and how optimal dosage is attained. However, a too lengthy discussion of side effects and possible toxicity would not be salubrious to an overly phobic or obsessional child. The promise of panaceas used to enhance the subjective anticipation of prompt results more frequently leads to disappointment and loss of confidence than to therapeutic gains. Nevertheless, parent and child must be instructed in the need for careful reporting of any effects that might occur and for sharing these results with the physician. The therapist who prescribes medication has to navigate skillfully the narrow course between Scylla and Charybdis.

OBSERVATION

Careful and frequent observation during the dose-regulating period will enhance confidence and diminish adverse responses—including fear—to early drug effects. The readiness of the physician to recognize minor behavioral changes as side effects and toxic signs is an important adjunct to helping establish optimal dosage, as well as to enhancing the therapeutic relationship. It has been clearly established that, as less developed poorly organized children gain control thanks to drug effects, their behavior and adaptation will improve to the delight of school and family.[1] On the other hand, children with more organized psychic structures who value their autonomy and sense of individual control may panic at minor degrees of sleepiness or a sense of mellowness, and will require more time to adapt. One child said, "I do better in school with the pill, but I don't like it because it makes me work."

PARENTS' REACTIONS

As important as the individual child's positive response may be in the process of drug administration, his family's participation is equally important. Psychoactive agents tend to provide too easy a means for assuaging destructive or regressive family needs. The family may want a quiet and obedient child when in actuality the child's full energetic responses may be necessary for enthusiastic learning. The results of administering medication may also be confounded with other difficulties, such as those characterized by toilet training and other demanding times and need for social control.

The interaction between mother and child may, indeed, replicate any prior phase of development and contaminate the present. The alert physician may intervene by careful and sensitive participation in the process because he understands better the drug-giving circumstance. For example, it is often possible to provide a child with more autonomy in administering his own medication if the mother can be made to understand that this is not a usurpation of her guiding role. Indeed, the occasion will provide an opportunity to discuss such maternal anxiety. Issues of premature autonomy for a child and symbiotic needs of a mother often become the focus of these explorations. The drug-administering-accepting circumstances may, on the other hand, be used as a focus for new reciprocity in a family, where doing for each other is not the predominant mode.

The child's family *must* also be considered a purveyor of community values. Members of the family may read or hear of the evil effects of the "drug scene." They may not necessarily have a clear distinction between unsupervised self-directed street drug use and medically directed therapeutic drug use. Public attitudes about priming children for later drug use or "doping" children of the lower class, rather than talking to them, have to be dealt with by understanding, education, and a tolerant grasp of the implications of using a physical means to modulate behavior or to modify mental states. Choice of the specific therapy for a particular child must be clarified, and enough time should be spent to convey the therapeutic indications, as well as to dispel public alarm. Sensitive inclusion of school personnel may be warranted if a midday dose is indicated. This requires the clinician to make a careful evaluation of the attitudes and understanding of other professionals and to maintain an assuring contact as a participant in the evolving therapy.

SUPERVISION AND CONTINUITY

The issues mentioned arise, return, and have to be dealt with at each stage of therapy. Effectiveness demands continuity of administration, which in turn requires continuing confidence in therapeutic work with child and families. One cannot function as a *deus ex machina* and start to give medication, arrive at a dose, and depend on its continued use without constant participation as long as the medication has to be taken. Thus, drug therapy amounts to a prescription for a therapeutic relationship until maximum drug effect is apparent, and also serves as adjunctive intervention on a continuous basis. Too often drug-giving can be looked at as a means of saving therapeutic hours. While one may have to see a patient less frequently and for less time if drug therapy is all that is indicated (and it seldom is), this is not the best milieu for medicinal administration. The family depends on the physician to distinguish among the pharmacologic agents, but the physician's job concerns more than choosing. He is called upon to supervise the process at each stage.

Once it has been decided that a medication is both effective and appropriate for a child, the more generic pharmacologic rules of thumb ought to be followed. The appropriate drug chosen for a particular child with a given symptom, which is the target for the desired effect, should be titrated to the appropriate dose of the agent for as long a time as is necessary to achieve a therapeutic effect.

Reference

1. Fish, B. and Shapiro, T. A typology of children in psychiatric disorders: I. Its application to a controlled evaluation of treat-

ment. *Journal of the American Academy of Child Psychiatry,* 1965, *4,* 32-52.

11
FAMILY THERAPY

The GAP report, *From Diagnosis to Treatment*,[1] described how the clinician plans treatment of a disturbed child and his family based on his diagnostic assessment, and includes an evaluation of the child's healthy functioning, as well as of the strengths and weaknesses of the family. The report emphasized that only an integration of the various facets of the child and his total life situation can provide a composite diagnostic appraisal, which in turn is necessary for appropriate treatment planning.

Little has been written about the effects of therapeutic work with the parents of a child seen in individual treatment. Even less is known regarding children's experience as participants in family therapy where diagnostic evaluation of individual family members usually does not occur or even is discouraged. Although most child mental health professionals expect some parental contribution to a youngster's psychopathology, they differ widely in what they expect of the parents in terms of their active participation in the treatment program beyond transportation and financial arrangements. This variation reflects different emphases on the importance of intrapsychic changes as a goal of therapy versus interpersonal and behavioral changes. A few therapists prefer not to know the parents, nor to have them report on the child. The majority try to take in the child, his parents, and surroundings as part of the treatment procedure, either through their own sessions with the parents or through the use of an intermediary co-therapist who regularly meets with the parents. Finally, the family therapist often insists on seeing all members of the nuclear family in his efforts at helping both the identified child-patient and his family cohort.

WORK WITH PARENTS

During the beginnings of child guidance work in our country in the 1920s, the emphasis was on individual therapy with the disturbed child. His parents' participation in treatment was mainly one of providing information and receiving advice. The impact of child psychoanalysis in the 1940s brought a shift of emphasis away from the environment, especially the family, toward the internalized conflicts of the child. The parents required help to permit and accept treatment of their child, but no major changes were expected of them. In other words, the parents became partners in permitting the intrapsychic therapeutic work to develop. Also, beginning in the 1940s, some child psychiatrists stressed the need for direct individual treatment of certain disturbed parents, with an emphasis on overcoming trauma and conflicts that had resulted in their experiencing poor parenting. More recently, psychodynamically oriented therapists often believe that therapeutic work, with parent figures, at various levels of intensity may result in improved parenting. "I refuse to believe that mothers need to change their personalities before they can change the handling of their child," wrote Anna Freud.[2]

Several components determine the process of the therapeutic supportive work with the parents of a child in individual or group psychotherapy. The chronological and developmental age of the child is of great significance for different kinds of parental participation in the treatment. Many preschool children with developmental problems can be helped by counseling with their parents. The basic premise for such successful work is the uniquely close relationship between the mother or caretaker and her under-five child, who is particularly sensitive to the mother's feelings and attitudes. A positive alliance between mother and therapist helps the mother to identify with the therapist in his understanding of the child. Psychotic, borderline, and markedly infantile mothers usually cannot utilize the therapist in this way; neither can the severely neurotic mother whose young child's symptoms have unconscious importance to her own early conflicts with parental figures. In such cases the mother often requires treatment herself.

The severity of the child's disturbance obviously influences the recommended therapeutic approach to the child and his family. The therapist may have to decide whether his patient can profit from the recommended treatment approaches while remaining at home or whether the child ought to be removed from his home. Developmental factors play a significant role. A neurotic reaction in a grade school child usually requires combined work with child and parents, while a neurotic adolescent might be successfully helped with a minimum of parental contact.

Common factors in working with parents

Although the process of working with parents in support of the child's therapy cannot be generalized due to the many variables operating in each individual family situation, some common aspects might be briefly recognized. During the early phase of treatment, the parents usually struggle with issues such as: What are the goals of treatment?; How does therapy work?; What do you (the therapist) expect of us in order for us to assist in our child's treatment?; How much of my own feelings and conflicts do I have to reveal?

When a child receives psychopharmacological treatment, the work with parents should aim at gaining the family's understanding of the need for medication, the need for supervision of drug administration, and the resolution of their fears about it.

Whoever works with the child's parents will be expected to provide explanations of their child's behavior in view of age-expected norms and of constitutional and temperamental varients. The child's symptoms, defensive maneuvering, and changes in family interaction must be discussed as treatment progresses. The goal for the therapist is to engage the parents as collaborators in the treatment of their child. This process emphasizes the importance of the parents readily reporting events and behavior of their child outside of therapy, their encouragement of him to bring certain material to the treatment sessions, their abstaining from questioning him about his therapy, and yet supporting therapy when he complains about its inconveniences. The parents may have to develop a tolerance for the temporary regressive and disturbing behavior of their child and be expected to cope with guilty, angry, and competitive feelings aroused by their awareness of their child's interaction with and dependence on his therapist. In an optimal collaborative situation, it is essential that both parents feel well informed about the progress of their child's treatment if it is to be successful.

CONFIDENTIALITY

Observing the confidentiality of the child's communications in therapy is an ongoing challenge to the clinician, regardless of whether the relationship is long-term or only a brief consultation. A flat promise to the child that the therapist will never relay any of the treatment communications to the parents can prove to be dangerous with, for example, a highly manipulative, risk-taking, or suicidal child. The child must understand that if the therapist needs to share some observations with the parents, he will inform the child in advance and explain his urgent reasons for this breach of confidentiality. In addition, many therapists find it of value to conduct occasional joint sessions with the child and the parents. During the sessions they discuss the therapeutic progress, hindrances, and other practicalities. Work with families requires continuous reassessment of the shifting equilibrium.

Some centers have reported considerable therapeutic success involving both father and mother in the treatment process of their child by utilizing group therapy with parents, running parallel with the treatment of the children.[3] After a while, such parent groups tend to change focus from the disturbed child onto family and marital relationships. As the cohesiveness of these groups develops, the parents can assist each other in verifying how faulty communication patterns and conflicts within the family have contributed to behavioral problems in their children.

Work with parents sometimes fails to overcome obstacles to the overall progress of therapy with a child. Resistances and transference conflicts may arise as the parents are reminded of their own childhood. The termination of therapy requires careful attention both to the outcome of the child's treatment and to the parents' ability to resume full parenting responsibilities. When the problems of their child have ended in only partial resolution, the parents are expected to adapt over time to the chronic burden of raising a mentally handicapped youngster. This is a taxing adjustment process for the whole family and often requires prolonged professional guidance and counsel.

WORK WITH FAMILIES

In trying to describe the therapeutic process of family group therapy, one is faced with the problem of a multitude of theoretical positions proposed by family therapists to account for their techniques with families. A previous GAP report, *The Field of Family Therapy*,[4] noted that family therapists tend to classify into two groups—those who view the family as complicating the psychic struggles of individual members and those who view the transactions of the family as determining, in a dynamic way, the responses and attitudes of its members. The report highlighted the need for "more theory behind family therapy." Present theories combine at least two bodies of knowledge: one-person dynamics and multi-personal system dynamics. The integration of these two conceptual systems into a comprehensive theory is a long-range task. The process of family diagnosis often overlaps with that of therapy itself. For example, many family group therapists find any effort to diagnose individual family members too impractical, restricting, and perpetuating of scapegoating.

Family therapists do agree that one ought not to treat the child separately from his family context. The child who is referred because of symptomatic behavior reflects conflicting forces acting within the family, and these forces interfere with the growth and individualization of the various family members. Thus, the entire family is viewed as the patient. The focus, therefore, for most family therapists, is on the immediate interpersonal manifestations of individual psychodynamics. Such manifestations are revealed through the communication patterns in the disturbed families. Consequently, the family therapist spends a great deal of time on the process of how information about facts and feelings is exchanged within the family, pointing out unclear statements, inconsistencies, and double messages, as in the following case example:

> Jane, eight years old, was more absent from than in school for two years. She was hospitalized for various complaints for which no organic cause was found. Her father had changed his work shift to afternoons to drive her to school when she was "well," and to take her home from school when she was feeling "sick" with various com-

plaints—headaches, nausea, stomachaches, sore throats, or fatigue. Eventually she was hospitalized in a pediatric hospital and no organic illness was found.

In consultation the therapist discovered that her parents fought constantly. Mother accused father of having numerous affairs at his place of work. He denied the accusations and related to his wife in a condescending and humorous manner, thus belittling her. Jane slept with her mother when father worked, because she was afraid to sleep alone. The therapist initiated therapy with the family, emphasizing that Jane was not physically ill, but she was responding to the family turmoil. Mother revealed that she had always felt inadequate and was afraid that father would abandon her. Father said he came from a background where men were expected to be "manly" but denied that he had affairs or would leave his wife. Jane said she never knew what was going to happen. Sometimes her parents were "nice" to each other and other times they were "mad," or "acted crazy." She never knew how they were going to act. She was confused and then felt "sick."

The therapist agreed that at times her parents acted "crazy" but it did not seem that they were going to separate and Jane did not have to enter into the "craziness." Jane was told the therapist was going to help her parents solve their problems. Sometimes she would see the family as a unit, see Jane alone, or see her parents together. As the confused messages and acting-out diminished, Jane discontinued sleeping with her mother and attended school regularly. Her symptomatic improvement occurred many months before her parents began to act less "crazy," since her parents were able to act on the therapist's advice to exclude Jane from their conflicts and assure her that they would stay married. Family therapy continued for the better part of a year, during which time the therapist continued to point out to the parents that they spoke and acted in confusing ways, and helped them to look at themselves and why they needed to behave as they did. Jane was asked to also look at what she was doing. With continued therapy

the unclear statements, inconsistencies, and double messages diminished.

HISTORY

Many generally accepted concepts and processes of family
therapy are based on Nathan Ackerman's work.[5] Ackerman
viewed the family as the natural bio-social unit on which
therapy should focus. The goal of therapy is to establish
communication and rapport among the family members, to
promote interpersonal competence, to clarify marital and
parental goals, to reduce scapegoating, and to "cultivate the
individual ego out of undifferentiated family ego mass."

The therapist is a participant observer, using his rapport
and empathy with the family members to catalyze the main
kinds of conflict and coping. In the process of family therapy,
the therapist: 1) clarifies the content of conflict; 2) fulfills the
role of a parent figure; and 3) serves as an educator.

Turning from Ackerman's view on the family process to
more contemporary formulations of family therapy as a
transactional process, the work of the Philadelphia Child
Guidance Clinic serves as an example.[6,7] The Clinic's family
therapists describe an intervention technique of "manipulation of the present" as the major tool for changing the family's
organization and functioning, leading to symptom removal
in the identified patient. The therapist wishes to intervene
as rapidly as possible, even in the first therapy session. This
implies that the diagnostic evaluation of the family interaction
evolves out of ongoing therapy. The therapist studies the
family as a set of persons interacting in various subsystems.
He recognizes, as he enters into the family constellation, that
he becomes part of a new system. The identified child patient
is viewed as caught in interactions between the other family

members, for instance, between his parents or between certain siblings.

Virginia Satir[8] has written about the technical process of involving young children in family therapy. Satir emphasizes that each member of the family, including even the young child, should be helped to report on what he sees, hears, feels, and thinks about himself and others in the presence of all family members. Even the symptom-free children are included in therapy, as they are important for maintaining the family homeostasis.

Some family therapists have made adaptations of traditional family therapy in order to become effective with disorganized low socioeconomic families.[9] Often these families are characterized by disconnected subsystems which perpetuate a marked discontinuity of behavior among individual family members. Thus, the therapist cannot expect consistency in the composition of the family group but has to accommodate to the fluid subsystems of the disorganized family. His therapeutic strategy involves manipulation of these family subsystems. Practically, this means holding separate sessions with members of the natural subgroupings, working toward sessions with the whole family. A major aim of the work with the subgroups is to sharpen the affective experience of the family members and promote meaningful interpersonal communication.

Most family therapists continue to agree with Ackerman that family therapy can be applied to practically all disorders as it is a "therapy of a natural living unit." Serious psychotic illness, sociopathy, and major progressive organic disease in family members have been mentioned as examples of the rare contraindications to including all members in family therapy.

References

1. Group for the Advancement of Psychiatry. *From Diagnosis to Treatment: An Approach to Treatment Planning for the Emotionally*

Disturbed Child. New York: Group for the Advancement of Psychiatry, 1973.

2. Freud, A. The Child Guidance Clinic as a center for prophylaxis and enlightenment. In J. Weinreb (Ed.), *Recent Developments in Psychoanalytic Child Therapy*. New York: International Universities Press, 1960, pp. 25-38.

3. Westman, J. C. and others. "Parallel Group Psychotherapy with the Parents of Emotionally Disturbed Children." *International Journal of Group Psychotherapy*, 1963, *13*, 52-60.

4. Group for the Advancement of Psychiatry. *The Field of Family Therapy*. New York: Group for the Advancement of Psychiatry, 1970.

5. Ackerman, N. W. *Treating the Troubled Family*. New York: Basic Books, 1966.

6. Haley, J. Family therapy—A radical change. In J. Haley (Ed.), *Changing Families: A Family Therapy Reader*. New York: Grune and Stratton, 1971, pp. 272-284.

7. Minuchin, S. *Families and Family Therapy*. Cambridge, Mass.: Harvard University Press, 1974.

8. Satir, V. *Conjoint Family Therapy: A Guide to Theory and Technique*. Palo Alto, Calif.: Science and Behavior Books, 1966.

9. Minuchin, S. and others. *Families of the Slums: An Exploration of Their Structure and Treatment*. New York: Basic Books, 1967.

12
GROUP THERAPY

As with dyadic therapy, the therapeutic process in a group
setting manifests itself in changing verbal and nonverbal con-
figurations during the course of a session. The group situation has often been compared to a projective test because
the material is alive and multidimensional and into it each
child must actively thrust his total personality. The more
actively the members participate in the process, the more
therapeutic change there is likely to be. The group process,
therefore, like the dyadic process, demands some effort,
work, and involvement on the part of the child. Moreover,
this means he must relinquish some magical-dependent-pas-
sive notions of treatment.

Process in the group setting can be observed best in the
following areas: 1) the patterns of communication; 2) the
nonverbal (affective, gestural) exchanges; and 3) "phenomenology."

PATTERNS OF COMMUNICATION

The therapeutic group creates its own structure and evolves
its own history. The children, it is true, bring in their own
personal histories, their own developments, and their prior
group experiences both inside and outside of their families.
When the "stranger group" begins, the members are un-
known to one another. The nonverbal behaviors of children
initially constitute the predominant communications within
the group. The nature and degree of the child's or adoles-

cent's disturbance will define his ability to interrelate and communicate. In any particular group, the many individual variations contribute greatly to the amount of process activity that evolves. Some children remain silent and isolated, while others may "hog the whole show."

Serial communications

A study of serial communications offers a good idea of the proceedings. As the group passes from being a leader-centered group with leader-directed communications and minimal interactional patterns to a group-centered group with group-directed communications and complex interrelational patterns, the process within the individual members begins to undergo change. From being isolated and unable to exchange ideas, for example, the child may at first enter into a paired relationship and conduct his whole therapeutic transaction within this "group of two." Subsequently, he may progress far enough to join a subgroup under the egis of some very active and dominant group member.

Toward the end of treatment, the child may begin to relate to the group as a whole and may even feel strong enough to monopolize the group discussion. The serial record may also highlight a talkative member's tendency to soliloquize rather than to communicate, or he may accept ideas from other members only when they duplicate his own line of thought. However, after experiencing a certain amount of genuine interaction, he may begin to consider ideas that are alien to his own. With further development, he may become better able to make new assimilations, so that an observable resolution of the egocentric structure of his inner thought processes may occur. Toward termination, he may demonstrate a number of communication changes. His verbal interactions may become increasingly plastic and modifiable by group experience. This readiness for verbal transactions is reflected in freer social and emotional responses to others.

As the group advances, the lines of communication between children tend to shorten and members begin to direct their remarks to the individuals for whom they are really intended. As an open forum is established, the group conductor no longer acts as a link between communications or as a catalyst for emotions. In this respect, the members themselves take over a great deal of the therapeutic activity of the therapist.

NONVERBAL EXCHANGES

Verbal communication is the most desirable, therapeutically, since it increases the "shareability" of the group experiences and brings much of the latent material into consciousness. In addition, speaking is the most effective and efficient means of communication, so that, as the members' skills develop, the nonverbal modes become less prominent. But among younger children, activities may facilitate the ease of communication as play and sensorimotor acts are their natural method of expression. Children easily move back and forth between playing-out and verbalizing their thoughts and feelings. Nonverbal exchanges often precede verbal ones. Silent members may indicate their involvement in the group process by affective displays or by a few small gestures. In the group milieu, silence often speaks louder than words. In children's groups, as in adult groups, a silent member may latch on to an articulate member and allow the latter to speak for him. By the use of gesture, head-nodding or -shaking, a silent child demonstrates his collusion with the speaker.

Messages

In children's groups, free group associations often occur around some central preoccupation. The group gradually

establishes a common language and its range of direct communication is constantly enlarged and more precisely defined. Such communication is necessary if any therapy is to
take place and is closely linked with the therapeutic process
itself. The next step consists of submitting all communications
to the additional process of interpretation which means the
children will find the meaning of the content and interaction
of their group. A great many hidden messages are trans-
mitted in the group and at first many are not "received" and
thus not responded to. As the understanding of manifest and
latent process increases, more and more of the messages
reach their destination and exert their influence. Even at its
best, the communications network within the children's
group has "holes" within it that often become foci of disturbance.

GROUP PROCESSES: A HALL OF MIRRORS

The ongoing process in the group reveals phenomena pe-
culiar to that group situation. These group-specific processes
include mirroring by means of which the individual's sense
of self, or identity, is refined. The group situation has been
likened to a "hall of mirrors" where an individual is confronted with various aspects of his social, psychological, or
body image. By a careful inner assessment of these aspects,
he can achieve in time a personal image of himself not grossly
out of keeping with the external and objective evaluation.

A number of group processes can be characterized phe-
nomenologically. The "condenser" reaction describes the
sudden discharge of deep and primitive material following
the pooling of associated ideas in the group. It is as if the
"collective unconscious" acted as a condenser covertly storing
emotional charges generated by the group and then discharging them under the stimulus of some shared event.
These "chain" reactions have a certain similarity to the free

associations of psychoanalysis and have the same capacity for penetrating unconscious strata. It may begin with a "free-floating" discussion and then suddenly, at a certain tense moment, some condenser theme is released and very soon each member may bring an association to the theme, for example, a fear of being laughed at, of being abandoned, or of being victimized. The "resonance" reaction is sometimes seen when individuals within the group at different stages of psychosexual development reverberate, each according to his own level, to some common stimulus.

Other processes within the group include pairings, subgroupings, silences, scapegoating (a fairly frequent process in latency aged groups), stranger reaction with the advent of new members, and struggling for deputy leadership or a special relationship with the therapist.

A vulnerability to certain emotions and expressions are especially marked in children's group processes, for example, voyeurism and exhibitionism, sadism and masochism, activity and passivity, homosexuality and heterosexuality, and elation and depression. These reactions often occur in paired situations, with one member of the pair complementing the other. The group as a whole may subdivide in terms of progressive and regressive forces, so that the two processes occur in the same session and lead to conflict, which in turn begs for resolution. The group therapist needs to be aware of group processes occurring in the group and to focus on the one or two that are most influential at any point, regardless of whether the manifestations are verbal or nonverbal.

13

THERAPEUTIC REQUIREMENTS OF ANY MILIEU

A group home, classroom for the emotionally impaired, residential treatment facility, therapeutic nursery, day treatment center, and foster home are only a few of the settings in which children and adolescents are placed with the hope that the milieu itself will have a therapeutic effect.

The physical settings of these facilities and the specific populations they serve vary greatly, yet there are many elements which must be common to all milieus if they are to be therapeutic. Preparation for placement is the initial phase of treatment and except in emergency situations should be adhered to. The child and family should visit the facility. Prior discussions with the child and family about their feelings can help them accept placement and tolerate the separation. Parents who have not had an opportunity to air their concerns might be more likely to yield to the child's pleas to take him home soon after he is placed, or to agree with the child's complaints about the staff or program.

The laws in several states mandate that older children and adolescents have their rights read to them. They are not subject to involuntary admission unless they are dangerous to themselves or others. Under these circumstances, they should understand that they need not participate in the treatment program and are free to leave the residence when they desire. These children or adolescents have the right to agree or refuse to participate in treatment. Clear understanding of the conditions of treatment tends to diminish the frequency of severe resistance, premature discharge, or, in the case of couples, elopement. Even when anger and resistance are high and overt cooperation is minimal, as in court-mandated placements, the staff should be supportive and be able to clarify the issues involved.

PERSONNEL

The personnel in any milieu are the setting's vital force. Preliminary orientation, continuing inservice training, conferences, and ease of informal communication among all personnel form the matrix of a treatment program. A staff member must be a humane and caring person who has a desire to help children and adolescents in need, but this alone is not sufficient. Understanding of developmental needs and the meaning of behavior and psychopathology are also essential. The needs of preschoolers, grade school children, and adolescents differ, as do the manifestations of their disturbances. Knowledgeable staff members are aware that children will relate to and identify with them, in addition to forming transference relationships with them. Maturity and self-awareness on the part of staff are required to interact appropriately and in a therapeutic manner with the children and one another.

Stresses among personnel are lessened if there is a common basis for understanding the children and when differences are communicated freely. Open communication minimizes opportunities for acting out by staff and children, and allows staff persons to direct their energies toward therapeutic endeavors. Professional identities, personal philosophies, and questions of status and authority are issues which are present in any group, and the group of individuals who are part of the therapeutic milieu must confront these issues as they arise. If the questions are raised in open discussion, there are possibilities for resolution, compromise, and understanding.

When the philosophy of the milieu does not permit open discussion but, rather, a strict hierarchy and procedure of operations exist, the resulting milieu will be sterile, ossified, and impersonal. Within this structure, there are possibilities for chronic anti-therapeutic activities by staff and children with periodic acute episodes of disruption during which tensions are high and opportunities for discharge of these tensions exist. Unresolved conflicts among the staff may be displaced onto the children and their parents, and therapeutic endeavors suffer.

PROGRAM

The program of a milieu must be addressed to the developmental, psychotherapeutic, recreational, and educational needs of the children. Programming the daily routine is at least as important as planning individual therapy hours. The therapeutic impact of all activities should be considered, including mealtime, privileges, bedtime, recreation, discipline, and staff interaction with individual children. Individual treatment plans, which can be altered when required, are essential. Home visits may be prescribed for some children and not for others. One child may require a structured program, another more flexibility and encouragement, and a third may need permission to give up pseudo-mature behavior and act like a child.

A meaningful and effective group and recreational program does more than just keep children busy. Individual and group activities provide opportunities for healthy competition and the development of feelings of competence. Many children, particularly in these settings, have low self-esteem, fear of failure, and are "poor losers." They may have made an art of doing nothing and, as a result, do not know how to do anything. Embarrassed by their lack of skills, they avoid participation in any activity. Thoughtful educational and recreational programming is necessary to involve them in activities in which they have previously failed; they also need to become involved in arts, music, and crafts in a positive manner so that fear of failure will be minimized and opportunities for success enhanced.

Community resources

The program also includes the community's resources and services. A program may have a clinician who works with the child and parents before the child is in the milieu, or a clinician in the community may have this task. Satisfactory communication and mutually understood working arrangements are essential for the staff of the milieu and clinicians in the community in order to help the family and to avoid distortion and misunderstanding. This is especially so when the child is in residence some distance from the home and the parents are working with a therapist in their area. When the child is discharged from the program, the therapist might continue to work with the family as continued therapy is frequently indicated.

A residential program may require the services of educational and recreational resources in the community. To implement these services, good communication and community education are required. Day treatment programs and group homes also have need of community resources and services. The staff should be prepared to deal with children whose behavior does not conform to community norms and to create an atmosphere of ready acceptance of these children into the community. In a situation where satisfactory and frequent dialogue occurs, the inevitable disruptions that occur in working with disturbed children can be weathered by the community. With the passage of time, members of the community often volunteer their services and, after an orientation program, volunteers can make important contributions to the treatment program.

The milieu requires a suitable physical environment, appropriate to the developmental and therapeutic needs of the children, although a less than ideal setting may be compensated for by dedicated professional staff and creative programming. Deficiencies such as structural or architectural defects, which may compromise the safety and security of the children, must not be allowed, but other defects can also make it difficult for therapy to take place.

The children and adolescents in any program must be seen as individuals, though they will share some common elements. The quality of the regular staff is most important and all must work together, each respecting the other. The institution must be seen as an extension of the community to which the child will return. Every attempt should be made to maintain meaningful communication and integration among all parts of the program, with one individual acting as the coordinator of all facets of the environment so that the child will always have an advocate, thus assuring maximum help.

14

COLLABORATIVE THERAPY WITH CHILDREN

Collaborative therapy may be defined as the psychological treatment of a child and his family carried on simultaneously by two or more professionals. Beginning in the 1920s, the team of child psychiatrist, psychologist, and psychiatric social worker was standard at child guidance clinics. Subsequently, collaborative modes of therapy became the rule on inpatient units, but less common in private practice. However, as Ornstein[1] stated:

> With a few notable exceptions, the limited amount of writing which has appeared on the process of collaborative therapy has appeared in the casework literature rather than the psychiatric.

Although collaborative work with children may take a number of forms, there are traits that are common to all. The key to successful collaborative therapy is free and open communication, and there must be an effort to apply the information obtained to understanding the child's psychopathology and to ongoing planning. Take the case of Susan and Sharon:

> Susan and Sharon, identical twin 12-year-old seventh graders, were referred by their pediatrician to the child psychiatry department of a children's hospital for treatment of anorexia nervosa. Several months before, both girls had begun to diet excessively, refused to leave their mother except to go to school, and became increasingly hyperactive. They were very anxious about their school-

199

work, which had always been excellent, and studied excessively. At the time of referral, Susan's weight had gone from 62 pounds to 52 pounds, and Sharon's to 48 pounds. The girls dressed identically and seldom separated. They were extremely dependent on their mother, who performed many of their daily grooming activities for them. Both parents were the youngest of large families who had sacrificed their personal goals to take care of ill parents. Susan and Sharon had three older brothers, ages 13, 14, and 15. The entire family verbalized the importance of family closeness and avoidance of disagreement.

Susan and Sharon were each assigned for individual psychotherapy to a psychiatric resident—Susan to a female and Sharon to a male. The parents were seen collaboratively by a psychiatric social worker. The residents quickly became aware of the twins' and the parents' expectations that the girls would be treated identically as their parents had always done. The residents initially found themselves each trying to guess what the other would do or say, and trying to avoid differences in the treatment. At Christmas, each sister brought her therapist a present. This had not been anticipated, and no plan had been made for dealing with the event. Each resident tried anxiously to figure out what the other would do, so the girls could be treated equally. At the end of the hour, Susan's therapist declined, while Sharon's therapist accepted the present. This fortuitous occurrence demonstrated to the family that the twins could be treated as individuals. In their next meeting, the therapists decided to use their own differences in personality and therapeutic style in working with Susan and Sharon.

A second major issue was competition. The two residents were peers and close friends and had some difficulty acknowledging their professional feelings of rivalry. As Susan and Sharon began to differentiate from each other, each made concerted efforts to enlist her therapist as an ally in the competitive struggle with her sister. In collaboration meetings, both residents were tempted to think or say, "My twin's getting better faster than your twin," or, "Your twin's causing my twin all the trouble." This became particularly difficult when Susan resumed eating several weeks before Sharon. When he wondered whether this meant that his colleague was a "better" therapist, Sharon's doctor was able to console himself with the fact that "his" twin had demonstrated more psychopathology and weight loss initially.

The psychiatric social worker provided considerable support for the parents, initially providing reassurance concerning the girls' medical status and subsequently encouraging them to treat each girl as an individual. The parents would have preferred harmonious similarity, with no competition or disagreement. The social worker was able to help them understand that Susan and Sharon needed to argue and to compete to develop normally.

As the case developed, issues of separation and individuation became of far greater importance than the eating. The treatment progressed fairly rapidly to a successful conclusion in six months, in large part because the child therapists were able to collaborate intensively and honestly and to use and respect their own similarities and differences to help Susan and Sharon. At a two-year follow-up, Susan and Sharon were both attractive, slender teenagers with different but equally stylish outfits and haircuts. Neither felt pressured to always agree or to always disagree simply to prove separateness, as they had previously. Both were performing extremely well in all areas.

SOURCES OF STRESS

Collaborators may be of the same discipline, but more often they are from different disciplines. This raises the specter of rivalry and prejudice between professionals:

> Tommy, a six-year-old only child of divorced parents, was referred to a child guidance center by his mother, a caseworker in a social welfare agency. She complained that

Tommy was having trouble adjusting to his parents' marital separation 10 months earlier and was disobedient, manipulative, hostile, and prone to temper tantrums. He had resumed wetting his bed at night and complained of abdominal pains. He had been diagnosed as having learning disabilities in school and often fought with his classmates. He was described by the assessing clinician as being an anxious, sad, but quite active and verbal child. Tommy was assigned for individual psychotherapy to Dr. Jones, a resident in adult psychiatry, as his first child psychotherapy case. Dr. Jones was being supervised by a senior child psychiatrist in private practice, who was also male. Tommy's mother was assigned to Ms. Smith, a senior staff social worker.

Initially, Dr. Jones, who was used to more verbal adult psychotherapy patients, was quite frustrated with Tommy. Although Tommy was quite willing to play with Dr. Jones and to superficially discuss his daily activities, he firmly denied that he had any "problems." Tommy's mother would often bypass her therapist and call Dr. Jones on the phone or corner him in the waiting room to report on Tommy's "bad" behavior. Each time this would happen, Tommy would react by refusing to talk in the subsequent therapy session. After six months of treatment, a joint meeting was held between the mother, her therapist, and Dr. Jones to attempt to clarify the lines of communication and confidentiality. The mother reported that she felt Tommy was not progressing and she felt "left out of" his therapy. She wanted more feedback on the process of his sessions. She also complained that Tommy had difficulty expressing his anger with his doctor. In fact, Tommy was quite adept at displaying his anger, although he was not able to talk about it. The mother herself had far more difficulties in the expression of anger, not only with her therapist and Dr. Jones, but in her everyday life.

As Tommy began to show an increasing ability to express his feelings verbally, his mother became uncomfortable with his more assertive stance. She began to request a reduction in the frequency of her appointments. She often arrived late or not at all, which meant that Tommy also missed all or part of his session. During this period of time, the mother began to talk with Ms. Smith of her generalized difficulty in establishing close relationships. When she found herself becoming close to anyone, she would immediately withdraw. This tendency became apparent in her therapy as well. Although the mother was quite knowledgeable about the facts and skills of child management, her fear of forming an attachment to her therapist was interfering with her functioning as a mother. In order to address this issue, the mother's sessions began to resemble individual psychotherapy more than child-centered parent counseling. Dr. Jones, reporting this to his supervisor, discovered that his supervisor strongly disapproved of social workers doing "individual psychotherapy." Dr. Jones was thus caught between his collaborator and his supervisor. In addition, Dr. Jones was becoming increasingly discouraged by Tommy's frequently missed appointments. He felt that it was the social worker's job to "make mother do the right thing" and bring Tommy for his sessions. Ms. Smith felt that confronting the mother more vigorously on this issue would not be helpful. More and more, Dr. Jones would complain to his supervisor about his difficulties with his collaborator, which the supervisor would exaggerate even further. Unfortunately, Dr. Jones was unable to discuss these openly with his collaborator.

The situation came to a head when the supervisor reported in a meeting with the clinic director that Ms. Smith was "ruining the case." Subsequently, the clinic director was able to arrange a treatment conference between Dr. Jones, Ms. Smith, and another child psychiatrist. At this time, the issues were thoroughly discussed. Since Tommy had made a great deal of symptomatic improvement, a decision was made to terminate the therapy. The case was closed after 16 months of therapy. Tommy was no longer enuretic or a behavior problem at home or school. He was learning at

the level of his potential. He had learned that it was permissible to be angry and to express those feelings verbally,
rather than in behavior. In fact, Tommy had become much
better than his mother at doing this. It was recommended
to the mother that she might wish to seek individual psychotherapy to deal with her own problems. She declined
to do this, however.

This vignette illustrates a problem in collaborative therapy:
the potential for aligning into competitive "teams" with the
child and his therapist on one side and the parent and his
therapist on the other. When one of the therapists is a trainee,
this adds the possibility of a supervisor joining one of the
"teams." In this case, the mothers pathology stirred up issues
relating to the genders, the disciplines, and the relative sen-
iority of the therapists. Administrative intervention was required to clarify the lines of communication and allow a
moderately successful conclusion.

Such difficulties may be minimized if each collaborator is
informed about the other's theoretical framework, experience, and preferred techniques. It should be noted that differences within disciplines may be as great as or even greater
than those between different disciplines. The ability of
professionals to form an alliance is more important than the
disciplines to which they belong. The community mental
health movement has tended to blur role definitions. It is
important that each collaborator understand his own function and what he can and should contribute that is unique
in a particular case. Perceived differences in status of the
different disciplines affect the family's relationship to the
therapists, thus undermining therapy. With unfortunate frequency, parents feel that they are being slighted because they
are being seen by a social worker while their child is being
seen by the doctor. Often, because of his unique experience
with life-or-death situations and his knowledge of both the

biological and mental aspects of behavior, the physician is the head of the treatment team. Third party payers and legislation covering practitioners hold the physician accountable for the actions of the team.

All aspects of the patient-therapist relationship influence collaborative therapy, and the problems are multiplied exponentially with each added patient or member of the therapeutic team. Take the following case:

> Antonio, a five-year-old boy living with his parents and three older siblings, was referred to a child guidance center at the urging of his school teachers. Everyone in his environment complained of his overactive behavior and short attention span. He was often aggressive with other children in school. His rapid speech and immature articulation made it difficult for him to make himself understood. He had been treated a year earlier with a psycho-stimulant with resulting exacerbation of his hyperactivity. His mother reported that her 14-year-old daughter was a behavior problem and her 11-year-old daughter had a history of hyperactivity previously treated with medication. The father was reported to be of little help in managing the children.
>
> Following the evaluation, Antonio was seen by a staff child psychiatrist for initiation of medication. On quite small doses of a dextroamphetamine compound, Antonio became increasingly active at home with significantly decreased appetite. His fighting in school increased. This reaction only intensified the mother's previously negative feelings towards medication, and the medication was stopped in June, to be attempted again in the fall. At the same time, the case was assigned to a psychology intern to provide individual play therapy for Antonio and child-centered parent counseling for his mother. This continued for two months with little progress, then the psychology intern left the clinic in the fall. The therapist had been able to facilitate Antonio's placement in a small, highly structured

classroom for children with emotional disturbances. She visited the class and consulted with the teacher on several occasions.

Antonio was then assigned to a group of boys and girls, ages six and seven, led by a staff movement therapist and a psychology intern. The mothers of these children met in a group of their own, led by a social work student. Antonio and his mother were seen again by the same staff child psychiatrist for another trial of stimulant medication. All four clinicians collaborated on a weekly basis. Antonio was begun on a very low dose of the original medication, which was titrated slowly. He and his mother were seen weekly by the child psychiatrist. During this period of time, Antonio was able to make little therapeutic use of his group, running from activity to activity and being unable to relate to others in a positive manner. His mother received negative feedback from her own mother and her friends on both her attendance at the clinic and Antonio's treatment with medication. Two months were required before Antonio was stablized on an appropriate dose, and his behavior improved at home and at school. At this time, mother began to see medication as the "only" answer and attempted to withdraw herself and Antonio from their respective groups. Since the mother continued to have significant difficulties in child management, and Antonio had exceedingly few social or play skills, the child psychiatrist insisted that they continue to attend therapy in order to receive medication at the clinic. The group therapist expressed some resentment towards the child psychiatrist, since the mother had been very clear in her expression of her view that the medication provided by the child psychiatrist was the most important factor in treatment.

Gradually, both Antonio and his mother became involved in their respective groups. At times, however, Antonio would complain to his mother that he didn't like group and didn't want to come. He did not report this to his therapist, and mother chose to complain to the child psychiatrist. Again, the child psychiatrist had to be firm about attendance at therapy, and relayed these concerns to the group therapist. After several more weeks, Antonio began to be able to make good use of group, attempting to play with the other children and to talk about his feelings. By the end of the school year when the groups terminated, both Antonio and his mother had made significant gains. Further therapy was not recommended. They continued to see the child psychiatrist for maintenance of Antonio's medication and collaboration with his school.

Members of the therapeutic team may themselves be tempted to act out conflicts between them. These may include competition between disciplines, systems problems, or individual incompatibilities. In turn, the child's therapist must avoid over-identification with the child and hostility toward the parents. This applies equally to the parents' therapist. The temptation to be a therapist for one's team collaborator must also be avoided. The simplest decision, such as in whose office to meet for collaboration, can become a symptom of the difficulties being experienced by the collaborators.

Issues in training

There are two particular areas of stress and conflict for trainees. Gaukler and Wannemacher[2] addressed one, the issue of the first-year psychiatric resident as leader of the treatment team in an inpatient hospital setting. While it is clear to the resident and to his co-workers that he is the least experienced of the team, he is in a position of leadership, especially vis-à-vis the family. Support and education from both supervisors and collaborators are therefore necessary to allow the resident an opportunity to fulfill this role.

Ireland[3] discussed another issue: treatment management problems in the collaboration between child psychiatric residents and psychiatric social workers. Areas of difficulty include deciding on the mode of treatment and the timing of conferences, and the resident's awareness of the impact on the parents and the child of, for example, appointment changes, contacts between the doctor and outside agencies, psychological testing, and waiting for appointments.

She described the problems that arise if the child psychiatrist talked with parents without consulting or informing the social worker. Ireland suggested that the problem is due to the traditional medical practice of focusing primarily on the patient rather than the environment. The collaborator may become aware before the resident's supervisor does whether or not the resident is stimulating competition between the parents and himself as to who is the better parent. He may have an overly authoritative attitude, be easily manipulated by parents, over-identify with the child, or make unrealistic demands on the parents without considering the realities of their situation. Ireland believes the skilled psychiatric social worker is in an ideal position to help parents, as well as teach the resident to make optimum use of community resources.

The most complex example of the problems of collaborative therapy is probably found in the inpatient child psychiatry unit, where child psychiatrist, psychologist, social worker, nurse, child care worker, teacher, and adjunctive therapists must work in a coordinated way toward distinguishable but shared goals. Boatman[4] discussed the situation of a severely regressed teenage girl who was admitted to an inpatient unit where she had previously been treated with moderate success. Against staff advice, she had been discharged by her parents. After her readmission, she failed to improve.

The staff closely examined the process of this girl's treatment, and isolated a number of factors which seemed to be contributing to their lack of success. The child psychiatry resident had previously held a position with more authority, and had also treated aggressive rather than withdrawn chil-

dren. She had ambivalent feelings about her return to training status and the change in the type of patient. An additional
conflict arose when a new assistant director of the unit was
appointed, who was initially seen as a threat to the resident's
status and authority on the unit. The mother's therapist, a
junior psychiatric social worker, had recently finished her
training. She was both pleased and fearful about filling a
clinical position on a ward with such seriously ill children.
There was a difference of opinion between the director of
the child psychiatry division and the director of social services
as to whether interviews held by the psychiatric resident and
by the psychiatric social worker served the same or different
functions. The social worker perceived herself as caught between these two authority figures, and it affected her work
with the mother. Another resident, who was the father's therapist, was struggling with competitive feelings with his pred-
ecessor.

The nursing staff was under stress because of an increase
in the number of severely disturbed young children on the
unit, and a simultaneous decrease in staff due to illness and
the holiday season. The head nurse, who had taken considerable interest in this young female patient during her prior
admission, was planning to resign, but had not shared this
with her staff. The other nurses noted her decreased spon-
taneity and interest, and resented the increased work for
them. They tended to act out their resentment in their contacts with this very difficult patient. Staff members seemed
to compete to be first to bring good news of the treatment
to the director. Unfortunately, this meant omitting certain
information that seemed indicative of a worsening of the
condition. A major conference of all the staff was organized.
A detailed examination of the girl's treatment, plus individual
supervision, finally enabled the staff to reach an understanding of the process and to remedy it. When the staff was able

to function in a more mature and integrated way, the patient was able to do the same.

Co-therapy of a child and/or family by more than one therapist brings up other issues. Communication is not as great a problem, since both participate simultaneously. It is more important, however, that the co-therapists have a good working relationship with the right combination of difference and sameness between them. *Conflicts over power and authority need particular handling.*

In collaborative therapy, as well as in collaboration with other professionals, a most crucial issue is the sorting out of confidential information from that which is important or essential for others to know. The child psychiatrist often functions as part of a team whose members are actively involved with the child continuously, although not all are doing "therapy." The treatment of school phobia is an example of therapy in which the child psychiatrist must coordinate a group that might include a psychiatrist, social worker, teacher, principal, and truant officer. As the number of professionals and the amount of their involvement increase, both the potential benefits and pitfalls multiply exponentially. Successful collaborative therapy requires an understanding of oneself and one's colleagues, as well as of the patient and family; otherwise, the recipients of this care may suffer needlessly.

References

1. Ornstein, A. Making contact with the inner world of the child: Toward a theory of psychoanalytic psychotherapy with children. *Comprehensive Psychiatry*, 1976, *1*, 3-36.
2. Gaukler, R. J., and Wannemacher, E. S. Collaborative process with psychiatric residents. *Social Work*, 1958, *3*, 83-88.
3. Ireland, E. The social worker's contribution to training in child psychiatry. *Journal of Child Psychology, Psychiatry and Allied Disciplines*, 1967, *9*, 99-104.

4. Boatman, M. J. and others. Can conflicts in collaborative therapy exacerbate psychosis? In S. A. Szurek and I. N. Berlin (Eds.), *Clinical Studies in Childhood Psychoses*. New York: Brunner/Mazel, 1973, pp. 654-673.

INDEX

Abreaction, 104-106
Ackerman, N., 184, 185, 186n.
Acting out, 31, 67, 183
  of parental wishes, 97
  of sexuality, 139
Adler, H., 34
Adolescence, 27, 137-47
  biological changes in, 137-38
  cognitive development in, 141-47
  early phase of, 140
  ego in, 139
  late phase of, 140
  middle phase of, 140
  and preadolescence, 138-39
  psychosocial development in, 138-40
  transference in, 143
Age, importance of, 75, 90
Aggression, 205-10
  as defense, 113
  identification with aggressor, 113
  in therapy, 109-10, 112
Allen, F., 31, 44n., 68, 110, 119n.
Alliance, therapeutic, 53
  in collaborative therapy, 204
Altruism, 132
Ambiguity, tolerance of by therapist, 69
Amnesia, 114
Amphetamine (Benzedrine), 40, 41
Anna O. case, 24
Anniversary reactions, 114
Anorexia nervosa, 199-200
Antiquity, child treatment in, 9-10
Anxiety, 153, 164
  and interpretation, 118
  and memory, 115, 116
  and play, 85, 103
  and sickle-cell anemia, 81-82
  and unfamiliar situations, 97-98
Aries, P., 11, 43n.
Aristotle, 24
Asthma, 157

Attentional deficit disorders, 162
Attitudes of therapists, 63
Autism, infantile, 32-33, 115
  etiology of, 125
Autonomy of toddlers, 125
Autosuggestion, induced, and
  neurosis, 25
Axline, V.M., 31, 44n., 68

Bandura, A., 166, 170n.
Behavior modification. See Behavior
  therapy
Behavior therapy, 27, 37-39. See also
  Reinforcement
  forerunners of, 21
  therapeutic process of, 155-68
  ethical aspects of, 163-68
  therapist-patient relationship in,
    162-63
Behavior Therapy in Children (Graziano),
  162
Bekhterev, V.M., 38
Bellevue Hospital, 37, 41
Benadryl, 40
Bender, L., 41, 46n.
Benzedrine (amphetamine), 40, 41
Berkshire Farm Center and Services
  for Youth, 37
Bernheim, H., 23-26
Binet, A., 33
Biofeedback, 157-58
  and unconscious, 157-58
Birth, prematurity of, 122
Blanchard, E., 164, 170n.
Blos, P., 138, 148n.
Boatman, M.J., 208, 211n.
Body language, 99. See also Nonverbal
  communication
Bonnet, J.P., 18
Borderline disorders, 115, 135, 179
Boredom, 113
Bradley, C., 41, 45n.

Braid, J., 23
Brain waves, 157
Breuer, J., 24
Bugental, J., 61, 77n.
Burnham, W.H., 155, 168n.

Canon, H., 62, 77n.
Castration fears, 107
Cathartic mehod, 24
Changing conceptuum, 62
Charcot, J.M., 24
Charisma of therapist, 26, 77
Chicago Polyclinic, 33
Child guidance clinics, 27, 31-34
    team approach in, 33
Child mortality, 11
Child psychiatry, 27
Chlorpromazine, 40
Christianity. See also Religion
    and child treatment, 10-11
    and disease, 10
Classical conditioning, 39. See also
    Behavior therapy
Cleveland Jewish Orphan Home, 37
Cognitive development, 141-47
Cognitive style of therapist, 64-66
Coleman, J.V., 65, 78n.
Collaborative therapy, 199-210
    alliances in, 204
    and communication, 199-201, 204
    competition in, 200-201
    defined, 199
    stress in, 201-210
        and training, 207-10
Columbia University, 38
Combs, A., 64, 65, 77n.
Comenius, J.A., 13, 14, 18, 19, 43n.
Commonwealth Fund, 34
Communication:
    and collaborative therapy, 199-201,
        204
    and language, 98-102
    in group therapy, 187-90
        nonverbal, 189-90
        serial, 188-89
    and play, 100-101
Compazine, 40
Competition in collaborative therapy,
    200-201
Condenser reaction, 190

Conditioned reflex, 38
Confidentiality, 83
    and family therapy, 180-81
    and note-taking, 87
Confrontation, 118
Conn, J.H., 30, 44n.
Contracts, contingency, 163-64
Convulsions, 32
Coping techniques, 112
Co-therapy. See Collaborative therapy
Coué, E., 25, 26, 43n.
Countertransference, 68, 108-10. See
    also Transference
    positive, 72
Culture:
    importance of, 90-92
    and therapeutic situation, 82-84
Custody, 96
Cylert, 40

Darwin, C. 22, 43n.
Daydreaming, 16, 50
    and deprivation, 91
Deaf mutes, schooling of, 18, 19
De Chastenet, A.M.J. (Marquis de
    Puységeur), 23
DeMause, L., 11, 42n.
Demonology, 10
Denial, 113, 134
Dependency of toddlers, 125-26
Depression, 102, 105, 106, 142, 191
    cycles of, 113
    of mother, 125
Descartes, 19
Desensitization, 13. See also Behavior
    therapy
Deutsch, H., 138, 148n.
Developmental stages, 15
Dexedrine, 40
Dextroamphetamine, 205
Diabetes, 158
Diet, 15
Dilantin, 40
Dissociation, 24
Divorce, 57, 96
Dorfman, E., 31, 44n.
Dreams, 114, 132
Drugs. See Psychopharmacology
Dubois, P., 26, 27, 43n.
Dummer, E.S., 33

Dynamics of Therapy in a Controlled Relationship, The (Taft), 31

Education, compulsory public, 13
Ego, 127
  in adolescence, 139
  autonomous functions of, 131
  auxiliary, therapist as, 111
  and empathy, 71
  in family, 184
  identity of, 140
  and memory, 114
  observation of, 143
Egocentrism, 141, 144, 188
Elavil, 40
Electrodermal activity, 157
Electromyography, 157
Elisabeth von R. case, 24-25
Emile(Rousseau), 17, 18
Emma Pendleton Bradley Home, 37, 41
Emminghaus, H., 36, 45*n*.
Empathy, 4, 70, 121, 184
  defined, 71-72
  and ego, 71
  and sympathy, 71
Encopresis, 162
Enlightenment, child treatment in, 12-19
Enuresis, 38, 41, 162, 167
Environment, 90-91
Epilepsy, 41
Erikson, E.H., 138, 148*n*., 151, 152, 154*n*.
Ethics of behavior therapy, 163-68
Euphoria, 142
Exhibitionism, 191
Experimental psychology, 37-38
Extinction, 38
Eysenck, H.J., 155, 169*n*.

Family therapy, 47, 70, 102, 143-44, 177-85
  and confidentiality, 180-81
  co-therapist in, 177-78
  and parents, 178-80
Fantasy, 126
  and deprivation, 91
  and interaction, 3
  and interpretation, 154

and repression, 115
  sexual, 114
Field of Family Therapy, The (GAP), 181
Finances of therapy, 83
Flexibility of therapist, 69-72
Frank, J., 47
Free association, 25, 29, 190-91.
  See also Psychoanalysis
Freud, A., 28, 29, 30, 44*n*., 68, 178, 186*n*.
Freud, S., 22, 24, 25, 27-29, 31, 44*n*., 67
Froebel, F., 19
From Diagnosis to Treatment (GAP), 177, 185*n*.
Furor sanandi, 67

Galen, C., 10
Gaukler, R.J., 207, 210*n*.
Gender, importance of, 75, 90, 93-95
Genetics, 22
Goldiamond, I., 164, 170*n*.
Graf, M., 28
Graziano, A., 155, 162, 163, 169*n*.
Green, A.H., 123, 147*n*.
Greenson, R., 71, 78*n*.
Group for the Advancement of Psychiatry, 177, 181
Group therapy, 187-91
  communication in, 187-90
    nonverbal, 189-90
    serial, 188-89
  mirroring in, 190-91
Guidance, 15
Guilt, 84, 132, 153, 167

Haldol, 40
Hall, G.S., 33
Hallucinations, 92
Harrison, S.I., 75, 79*n*.
Hartmann, H., 117, 119*n*.
Hawthorne-Cedar Knolls, 36
Headbanging, 124
Healy, W., 33, 34, 45*n*.
Henry, G.W., 10, 42*n*.
Herson, M., 164, 170*n*.
Hippocrates of Cos, 10
Homeostasis in family, 185
Homosexuality, 191
Hyperactivity, 41, 157

Hypnosis, 22-27
  and catharsis, 24
  and hysteria, 24, 27
  physiological processes in, 23
Hysteria, 92, 128
  and hypnosis, 24, 27

Idealism of therapist, 62-63
Identification, 97, 126
  with aggressor, 113
  trial, 72
Identity, 138
  of ego, 140
*Idiocy and Its Treatment By the
    Physiological Method* (Seguin), 20
Illusion, therapeutic, 149-50
Imipramine (Tofranil), 40
Individual Delinquent, The (Healy), 33
Individual differences, 13
Individuality, 15
Individuation. *See* Separation-
    individuation
Infancy, 122-25
  superego in, 29
Infanticide, 9
Infant mortality, 11
Insight, 53-54
  and action, 56
  and unconscious, 53
Institute of Juvenile Research, 34
Intelligence, 41, 92-93, 167
  and language, 93
Interpretation:
  and anxiety, 118
  child acceptance of, 118
  and fantasy, 154
  and resistance, 118
*Introduction to the Technique of Child
    Analysis* (A. Freud), 30
Introjection, 134
Introspectionism, 38
IQ, verbal, 41. *See also* Intelligence
Ireland, E., 207, 208, 210n.
Itard, J.M.G., 19-21, 43n.

Jaffe, S., 39, 45n.
James, W., 33
Janet, P., 24, 26
Jessner, L., 68
Jewish Protecting and Aid Society, 36

Jones, M.C., 38, 45n.
Judge Baker Foundation, 34
Juvenile Court of Chicago, 33
Juvenile courts, 33, 36
Juvenile delinquency, 33-34

Kanner, L., 33
Kauffmant, M., 26
Keniston, K., 138, 147, 148n.
Kennel, H.H., 122, 147n.
Kern, S., 27, 44n.
Kindergarten, 127-30
Kings Park State Hospital, 37
Klaus, M.H., 122, 147n.
Klein, M., 28, 29, 44n.
Kraepelin, E., 32

Langford, W., 68
Language:
  and communication, 98-102
  and intelligence, 93
  and therapy, 82-83
Latency, 94, 133, 134, 137
  and activity, 103
Learning theory, 38
Lesser, G.S., 92, 119
Leukemia, 82
Levy, D.M., 30, 31, 44n., 68
Liébeault, A.A., 23
Limit-setting, 118
Lithium, 40
Little Hans case, 28
Locke, J., 13-19, 38, 43n.
London, P., 164, 170n.
LSD- 25, 40
Luther, M., 13

Magical thinking, 10, 112-13, 149, 151
Mahler, M., 125, 129, 148n.
Marriage, 181
  in Middle Ages, 11
Masochism, 191
Mateer, F., 155, 168n.
Maudsley, H., 36, 45n.
Maurois, A., 89
Mellaril (thioridazine), 40
Memory, 114-17
  and anxiety, 115, 116
  and ego, 114

Menarche, 139
Mental retardation, 19-22, 93, 97
  nineteenth-century care of, 35-36
Meprobamate, 40
Mesmer, F.A., 22, 23
Mesmerism, 23
Method of Persuasion, 27
Meyer, A., 33
Middle Ages:
  child treatment in, 10-11
  marriage in, 11
Middle childhood, 130-37
  sexuality in, 133-34
Milne, A.A., 130
Milner, M., 149, 150, 154n.
Minde, K., 122, 147n.
Minimal brain damage (MBD), 41
Mirroring in group therapy, 190-91
Modeling, 38, 39, 124, 158-62
Molitch, M., 41, 46n.
Montessori, M., 21-22
Moral treatment, 20
Motor behavior, 131, 157
Mowrer, O.H., 38, 39, 45n.
Mowrer, W.M., 38, 39, 45n.
Murphy, L.B., 112, 119n.
Mutuality, 4

Nacht, S., 65, 77n.
Nancy Clinic, 25-26
Narcissistic injury, 110
Navane, 40
Neugebauer, R., 11, 43n.
Neurosis, 179
  and autosuggestion, 25
  and therapist, 62, 63
  and unconscious, 25
New Haven Children's Community
    Center, 38
New Jersey State Home for Boys, 41
New York House of Refuge, 35
Non-Possessive Warmth Scale, 72
Nonverbal communication, 99, 101-
    103
  in group therapy, 189-90
Normal adolescence, 137
Northern Home for Friendless
    Children, 35
Notes on the Reality Principle
    (Hartmann), 117

Note-taking and therapeutic situation,
    86-87
Now We Are Six (Milne), 130
Nursery school, 127-30
Nurses, 209-10

Obesity, 86
Obsessions, 25, 128
  and drugs, 173
Oedipus Complex, 29, 107, 129
Oestereicher, S., 12
Olden, C., 71, 78n.
Omnipotent ideation, 149, 151
Operant conditioning, 39, 156-57. See
    also Behavior therapy
Organic brain disease, 41
Origin of Species, The (Darwin), 22
Ornstein, A., 199, 210n.
Orthophrenic Establishment, 21
Orthopsychiatry, 15
Overdetermination, 89-90

Paoli, C., 92, 119n.
Parents:
  and abreaction, 105
  and family therapy, 178-80
  and infants, 122-25
  initial contact with, 95-98
  and nursery school-kindergarten,
    127-30
  and psychopharmacology, 173-75
  and therapeutic situation, 83-84
  and sex roles, 94-95
  and toddlers, 12-27
  and transference, 107-108
  unconscious wishes of, 97
Parsons Child and Family Center, 36
Passivity, 191
  and play, 104
  of therapist, 64
  and transference, 107-108
Patterson, G.R., 161, 169n.
Pavlov, I., 38
Peer groups, 21, 136-37
Perceptual style of therapist, 64-66
Péreire, J.R., 18-19
Personality of therapist, 59, 61-77
  behavioral definition of, 63-64
  characteristics of, 66-77
  over-idealism in, 62-63

and perceptual and cognitive style,
    64-66
Pestalozzi, J.H., 19
Phenylzine, 40
Philadelphia Child Guidance Clinic,
    31, 69, 184
Phobias, 128
    behavioral treatment of, 38
    and drugs, 173
    of school, 210
Physiology and Pathology of the Mind, The
    (Maudsley), 36
Pinel, P., 19, 20
Placebos, 172
Play. *See also* Play Therapy
    and anxiety, 85, 103
    and communication, 100-101
    games, 16
    and passivity, 104
    and therapeutic process, 152-53
    valuation of, 13-14
Play therapy, 27-32. *See also* Play
    active (situational), 30
    non-directive, 31
    open-ended, 88
    structured, 30, 31
    and therapeutic situation, 84-86
Pleasantville Cottage School, 36-37
Poliakoff, S., 41, 46n.
Potter, H.W., 37, 45n.
Process, meaning of, 3-7
    and interaction, 3
    latent and manifest, 6-7
Projection, 113, 134
Prolixin, 40
Psychiatric hospitals, 34, 37
Psychiatric social workers, 207-209
Psychiatrists, 199-210
Psychiatry, dynamic, origins of, 22-27
Psychoanalysis, 27-28, 191
    and illusion, 150
    and internal conflict, 178
    therapeutic orientation of, 63
    and therapeutic zeal, 67-68
Psychoanalysis of Children (Klein), 28
Psychological Clinic, The (Witmer), 32
*Psychology from the Point of View of a
    Behaviorist* (Watson), 38
Psychopharmacology, 27, 39-41, 171-
    75, 179-80, 205-206

and meaning of medication, 171-72
and observation, 173
and parental reactions, 173-75
preparation for, 172-73
supervision and continuity in, 175
Psychosis, childhood, 37, 41, 115, 179,
    185
    and mental deficiency, 32
Puberty, 138. *See also* Adolescence

Race, importance of, 75, 90
Rank, O., 31, 65
Rapport, therapeutic, 23, 28, 31, 102,
    184
Rapprochement phase, 125
Rationality and passion, 15-16
Reaction formation, 107
Reality-testing, 97
Recall, 114-17. *See also* Memory
Referrals, 168
Reformatories, 35, 36
Regression, 126, 135, 180
    and drugs, 173-74
    resistance to, 139
    symbiotic, 125
Regurgitation, 124
Reinforcement, 164. *See also* Behavior
    therapy
    fixed-ratio, 157
    interval, 156-57
    random ratio, 156-57
Release therapy, 30-31
Religion, 92
    and child treatment, 10-11
    and healing, 10
    importance of, 75
Renaissance, child treatment in, 11-13
Repetition, 134
Repression, 24-25, 114
    and fantasy, 115
Reserpine, 40
Residential treatment centers, 34-37
Residents, psychiatric, therapeutic
    orientation of, 63
Resistance, 103, 151, 181
    and family situation, 83, 84
    and interpretation, 118
    to regression, 139
Respondent conditioning, 156-57
Ritalin, 40

Rogers, C., 31, 71, 78n.
Role model, therapist as, 87-88
Role-playing, 65, 158-62
Roman law on infanticide, 9
Rousseau, J.J., 12, 16, 17-19, 43n.
Ryther Child Center, 37

Sachs, H., 63, 67, 77n.
Sacrifice, religious, of children, 10
Sadism, 191
Satir, V., 185, 186n.
Scapegoating in families, 182
Schafer, R., 71, 78n.
Schizophrenia, childhood, 37, 41, 115
School of Infancy (Comenius), 13
Secondary process thinking, 139
Seguin, E., 18, 20, 21, 35, 36, 43n.
Selective participation, 61-62
Self beyond roles, 65
Self as therapeutic instrument, 64-67
Self-acceptance of therapist, 73
Self-assessment, 73, 154
Self-concept, 139
Self-esteem, 76, 94, 110, 139, 195
Self Mastery Through Conscious
    Autosuggestion (Coué), 25
Separation-individuation process, 124
  and clinging, 128, 129
  second phase of, 139
Sexism, 90
Sex roles, 93-95
  and socieconomic class, 94, 96
Sexuality:
  acting-out of, 139
  fantasy, 114
  in middle childhood, 133-34
  and transference, 143
Shaping, 158-62. See also Behavior
    therapy
Shapiro, M.B., 155, 168n.
Sibling rivalry, 30
Sickle-cell anemia, 81-82
Socio-economic class:
  importance of, 75, 90
  and sex roles, 94, 96
Sociopathy, 185
Solomon, J.C., 30, 44n.
Some Thoughts Concerning Education
    (Locke), 14
Somnambulism, 116

artificial, 23
Soper, D., 64, 65, 77n.
Southard School, 37
Spitz, R., 124, 147n.-48n.
State Custodial Asylum, 36
Stelazine, 40
Stodolsky, S.S., 92, 119n.
Strupp, H., 62, 63, 77n.
Stuttering, 117
Subconscious fixed ideas, 24
Suggestion, hypnotic, 23
Sullivan, H.S., 14
Superego, 105
  development of, 29, 140
Swaddling, 12, 15
Symptom substitution, 164-66
Synergic gratification, 75

Taft, J., 31, 44n.
Taractan, 40
Teething, 33
Television, 91
Temperament, innate, 15
Temperament and Behavior Disorders in
    Children (Thomas), 112
Temper tantrums, 159-61, 165, 166
Therapeutic process. See also
    Therapeutic situation
  and affects, 153-54
  of behavior therapy, 155-68
  in dyadic psychotherapies, 149-54
  microprocess and macroprocess in,
    152
  and play, 152-53
Therapeutic situation, 47-59. See also
    Therapeutic process
  analysis of problem and cause in, 51-
    52
  and cultural differences, 82-84
  explanation of situation in, 52-55
  formula for change in, establishment
    and implementation of, 55-57
  and illusion, 150
  limitations of, 81-82
  and note-taking, 86-87
  and personnel, 194-95
  and play therapy, 84-86
  and programs, 195-97
    and community resources, 196-97
  termination of, 57-59

and therapist as role model, 87-88
working relationship in, 48-51
Therapeutic zeal of therapist, 67-69
Thioridazine (Mellaril), 40
Thomas, A., 112, 119n.
Thorndike, E.L., 37-38
Tics, 117, 128
Toddler years, 125-27
Tofranil (imipramine), 40
Toilet training, 15, 38-39
Traitement Moral, Hygiène et Éducation
    des Idiots et des Autres Enfants
    Arrieres (Seguin), 20
Transference, 106-108, 150, 181. See
    also Countertransference
  in adolescence, 143
  and family situation, 83
  and passivity, 107-108
  and sexuality, 143
Trilafon, 40
Triperidol, 40
Truax, C., 72, 78n.

Unconditional positive regard, 72
Unconscious:
  and biofeedback, 157-58
  collective, 190-91
  and family situation, 83
  and insight, 53
  and neurosis, 25

of therapist, 63
University of Bern, 26
University of Pennsylvania:
  Psychological Clinic, 32
  School of Social Work, 31

Voisin, F., 21
von Hug-Hellmuth, H., 28, 44n.
Voyeurism, 191

Wannemacher, E.S., 207, 210n.
Warmth of therapist, 72-73
Watson, J.B., 38, 39, 45n., 155, 168n.
Weiner, J.M., 39, 45n.
Wet nurses, 11, 12
Whitehead, A.N., 3, 5, 6, 7n.
Wickes, F., 68
Wild Boy of Aveyron, The (Itard), 19
Wilking, V.N., 92, 119n.
Winet, R.A., 163, 170n.
Winkler, R.C., 163, 170n.
Withdrawal, schizoid, 41
Witmer, L., 32-34, 45n.
Wolpe, J., 155, 169n.
Wundt, W., 32

Yates, A.J., 155, 169n.

Zilboorg, G., 10, 42n.